The Strategic Data Playbook

A Six-Step Formula to Turn
Your Company into a Data-Driven Powerhouse.
Unlock Profits and Productivity with Advanced
Analytics and Artificial Intelligence.

Wissen Lau.

Copyright © 2024 by Wissen Lau.

All rights reserved.

No portion of this book may be reproduced in any form without written permission from the publisher or author, except as permitted by applicable local copyright law.

This publication is designed to provide accurate and authoritative information in regard to the subject matter covered. It is sold with the understanding that neither the author nor the publisher is engaged in rendering legal, investment, accounting or other professional services. While the publisher and author have used their best efforts in preparing this book, they make no representations or warranties with respect to the accuracy or completeness of the contents of this book and specifically disclaim any implied warranties of merchantability or fitness for a particular purpose. No warranty may be created or extended by sales representatives or written sales materials. The advice and strategies contained herein may not be suitable for your situation. You should consult with a professional when appropriate. Neither the publisher nor the author shall be liable for any loss of profit or any other commercial damages, including but not limited to special, incidental, consequential, personal, or other damages.

All trademarks, service marks, and brands mentioned or depicted in this publication remain the property of their respective owners. Their use is for illustrative and informational purposes only and does not imply any endorsement, sponsorship, or affiliation with this book, its author(s), or its publisher. Publication of these trademarks is without permission or backing from the trademark owners.

Published in the United States and the United Kingdom.

First Edition. 2024.

To my parents, William and Suzuya, for their unwavering support and encouragement. To my wife, Sarah, for her love and patience during these seven months of writing this book. And to my friends and colleagues for shaping my personal and professional growth.

Thank you.

Table of Contents

Introduction 1

Part 1: Foundations of Data Strategy 4

    Chapter 1: Understanding Data Strategy 5

        What Is Data Strategy? 6

        Key Components for a Successful Data Strategy 8

        Consequences of No or Poor Data Strategy: 10

        Introducing the Six-Step Data Strategy Framework 13

        Summary 16

    Chapter 2: Aligning Data Strategy with Business Objectives 18

        Why Aligning Data Strategy with Business Strategy Matters 19

        Understanding Business Strategy 19

        Types of Business Value 21

        Alignment Challenges 25

        Overcoming the Alignment Challenges 27

        Defining Business Objectives and Aligning with Data Strategy 29

        Summary 31

    Chapter 3: Assessing Your Data Maturity 32

        Step 1: The Emerging Stage 33

        Step 2: The Empowered Stage 39

        Step 3: The Integrated Stage 47

        Step 4: The Strategic Stage 54

        Step 5: The Visionary Stage 62

        Assessing Your Company's Data Landscape 68

Summary 75

Part 2: Building the Necessary Capabilities 77

   Chapter 4: Cultivating a Data-Driven Mindset 78

      Common Challenges 80

      Principle 1: Leadership and Advocacy 82

      Principles 2: Cultivating Data Literacy 88

      Principle 3: Trust and Transparency 95

      Summary 101

   Chapter 5: Empowering Your People 102

      Common Challenges 105

      Principle 1: Training and Education 107

      Principle 2: Talent Management and Retention 114

      Principle 3: Feedback and Recognition 121

      Summary 127

   Chapter 6: Developing Effective Processes 129

      Common Challenges 131

      Principle 1: Data Governance Principles 134

      Principle 2: Roles and Responsibilities 141

      Principle 3: Data Quality and Management 150

      Summary 157

   Chapter 7: Leveraging Technology and Tools 159

      Common Challenges 161

      Principle 1: Designing a Flexible Data Approach 164

      Principle 2: Making Informed Infrastructure Decisions 172

      Principle 3: Empowering Teams with Self-Service Analytics 181

      Summary 189

Part 3: Executing and Sustaining Your Data Strategy 192

Chapter 8: Developing and Implementing Your Data Strategy ..193
    Prioritising Your Data Initiative 194
    Defining Milestones and Deliverables 198
    Structuring the Data Strategy Implementation Plan 199
    Engaging Stakeholders and Governance Bodies 201
    Summary 202
Chapter 9: Measuring Success and Demonstrating ROI 204
    Establishing Meaningful KPIs and Metrics 206
    Case Study: Choosing the Right KPIs at ASOS 209
    Summary 210
Chapter 10: Future-Proofing Your Data Strategy 211
    Staying Ahead with Emerging Technologies 213
    Anticipating Regulatory and Market Changes 216
    Creating Enduring Value 220
    Summary 223
Conclusion 224
References 227
About the Author 238

Introduction

If your company is like many others, you're probably swimming in data but struggling to turn it into something that moves the needle. You might have endless reports collecting dust or entire teams generating charts and graphs that don't go anywhere. You want to see results: more revenue, cost savings, and streamlined processes. But, without a clear strategy, you may treat data more like a static storage project than a dynamic source of new opportunities.

What made the difference wasn't just the data itself. It's how effectively you can align information with your company's goals and create a culture that looks for meaningful insights and translates them into action. Over the past decade, I've worked with leaders in different industries to help them change how they think about data. I've seen that the most significant gains don't come from just collecting more data or buying the latest shiny tools. Instead, it's about crafting a logical, actionable strategy that fits your company's unique objectives. In other words, data leadership isn't about having more numbers; it's about using the right data to solve real problems, support the right teams, and reach the right outcomes.

This book will show you exactly how to do that.

The Objective of This Book

The Strategic Data Playbook will be your blueprint for using data to develop new opportunities and grow your company. You don't need to be an expert in data genius or tech wizard. By the time you finish reading, you'll know how to create a data strategy that matches your company's goals, weave data into the everyday fabric of your company, and build a workplace culture that values data-driven decisions. Instead of letting data pile up, you'll learn how to pinpoint, plan, and prioritize the initiatives that yield measurable, bottom-line benefits.

Throughout the book, you'll see methods that have worked in actual businesses. You won't get bogged down in technical jargon or academic theory. Instead, you'll learn how to show that your data projects are worth it, set up the right teams and processes, and choose tools that truly serve your goals.

What You Will Learn in Each Part

This book is divided into three main sections, each focusing on a part of the overall process of planning and developing a data strategy.

Part 1: Foundations of Data Strategy

In these chapters, you'll learn what a data strategy really means. We'll cut through the buzzwords and show you how to tie your data efforts to your core business goals. You'll learn the six step data strategy framework. You'll also learn how to measure your current 'data maturity' so you'll know where you stand before moving forward.

Part 2: Building the Necessary Capabilities

Here, we'll discuss what it takes to get everyone on board with using data. This includes helping leaders and staff think differently, making sure your team has the right skills, and setting up the best processes for handling data responsibly and ethically. We'll also consider choosing tools that make sense rather than just chasing the latest trend.

Part 3: Executing and Sustaining Your Data Strategy

The last part shows you how to put your plan into action. You'll learn how to roll out your data strategy step-by-step, measure what's working, show clear results to stakeholders, and keep improving over time. We'll also talk about how to stay ready for new technologies and future changes in the market.

Questions This Book Will Help You Answer

You might be asking yourself these questions:

- How do I build a data strategy tailored to my company's needs? (Answered in Chapter 1)
- How can I ensure our data initiatives deliver real business value? (Chapters 2 and 8)
- What steps should we take to increase our data maturity and leverage our existing assets more effectively? (Chapter 3)
- How do I foster a culture that embraces data, even among those resistant to change? (Chapters 4 and 5)
- What processes and governance models ensure data is both usable and trustworthy? (Chapter 6)
- How do I select and implement technologies that enable and not hinder our strategy? (Chapter 7)
- How do we measure the success of our data efforts and demonstrate ROI? (Chapter 9)
- What should we do to ensure our data strategy remains resilient and adaptable as market conditions shift and technology evolve? (Chapter 10)

By the end of *The Strategic Data Playbook*, you will have a straightforward, step-by-step approach to leading your company with data. You won't just understand what needs to be done; you will also know how to guide your team and company toward a stronger, more successful future driven by data-driven insights.

Part 1:
Foundations of Data Strategy

Chapter 1:
Understanding Data Strategy

Today's world is drowning in data but starving for insights. In my previous engagements, a director said, 'We have all the data we need already; we just need to surface the benefits from it.' Does that sound familiar to you? Many organisations sit on a goldmine of information, yet struggle to turn it into actionable strategies. In this chapter, we'll explore what a data strategy truly is, why it's essential for your business, and how it differs from traditional IT strategy. I'll share key components that make up a successful data strategy, discuss the pitfalls of neglecting it, including some real-world case studies, and introduce a six-step framework to guide you toward data-driven success.

What Is Data Strategy?

A data strategy is your roadmap for how your company collects, manages, and uses data to achieve its business goals. Think of it as a blueprint that aligns your data initiatives with your overall objectives. It's not just about technology; it's about turning data into a strategic asset that drives value.

Unlike one-off projects that address specific issues, a data strategy provides a holistic framework. It ensures that every data-related activity contributes to your broader business ambitions. It's about making data work for you meaningfully.

Key Components of a Data Strategy

A robust data strategy typically contains these four pillars:

1. **Mindset**: A cultural commitment to data-driven decision-making across all levels of the organisation.
2. **People**: The talent and leadership required to drive data initiatives effectively.
3. **Process**: The methodologies and governance structures that ensure data is managed consistently and responsibly.
4. **Tools/Technology**: The technological infrastructure that enables data collection, storage, analysis, and security.

These components work together to transform raw data into valuable insights that take your business to the next level. To truly leverage data and speed up business value through data analytics, artificial intelligence, machine learning, and generative AI, companies must address all four pillars together, ensuring a unified and comprehensive approach.

Data Strategy vs. IT Strategy

You might wonder, 'Isn't a data strategy the same as an IT strategy?' The short answer is no. While they overlap, they serve different purposes.

An **IT strategy** focuses on your company's technological backbone: hardware, software, networks, and cybersecurity. Its goal is to ensure your systems run smoothly and securely.

A **data strategy** is about leveraging data to drive business outcomes. It's less about the tools and more about how you use them to generate insights.

Let's take NHS Digital as an example. Launched in 2021, its IT strategy focuses on digitising patient records to improve accessibility and efficiency in healthcare. But what about its data strategy? It aims to enable faster and more accurate diagnosis using machine learning and personalise treatment plans through AI-driven analytics. While the IT strategy sets up the digital infrastructure, the data strategy leverages that infrastructure to generate actionable insights that enhance patient care.

The Strategic Value of Data as an Asset

Data is often called the 'new oil' because of its potential to fuel business growth and innovation. When treated as a strategic asset, data can help companies:

- **Enhance Customer Understanding**: By analysing customer behaviours and preferences, you can tailor your products and services to meet their specific needs, improving satisfaction and loyalty. For example, a personalised recommendation engine.
- **Make Smarter Product and Service Decisions**: Data-driven insights help you innovate and refine offerings based on

market trends and customer feedback. For example, new product development.
- **Improve Business Processes and Operational Efficiency**: Streamlining processes through data analytics can reduce costs and boost productivity. For example, improve utilisation of specific assets.
- **Boost Financial Performance**: Leveraging data can lead to better financial decisions, risk management, and forecasting. For example, allocate more resources to high ROI-advertising platforms.

Key Components for a Successful Data Strategy

Creating a successful data strategy is like building a house. It would help if you had the proper foundation and materials. Let's explore the essential components further.

Mindset:

A data-driven mindset is crucial. It involves:

- **Embracing Data in Decision**: Encouraging everyone to rely on data rather than gut feelings.
- **Promoting Data Literacy**: Training your team to understand and use data more effectively.
- **Fostering Curiosity:** Creating an environment where colleagues are encouraged to question the data and experiment with new ideas.
- When your company truly values data, making evidence-based decisions becomes second nature.

People:

Your data strategy is only as strong as the people behind it. This includes:

- **Leadership**: Executives who allocate resources, promote data efforts, and set the vision.
- **Data Professionals**: Data scientists, analysts, and engineers with the technical know-how.
- **Business Stakeholders**: Individuals who understand business needs and can translate data insights into actionable strategies.

A diverse team ensures that your data projects are technically sound and aligned with your business goals. More on this in the next chapter.

Process:

Consistent processes ensure your data is reliable and secure:

- **Data Governance**: Policies that dictate how data is accessed, used, and protected.
- **Data Quality Management**: Systems to ensure your data is accurate and up-to-date.
- **Agile Methodologies**: Flexible approaches allowing quick adaptations in a changing environment.

Standardised processes minimise errors, improve data security, and keep everyone on the same page.

Tools & Technology:

The right tools and technologies empower your people and processes.

- **Data Storage Solutions**: Databases, data lakes, and warehouses that store data efficiently and securely.
- **Analytics Platforms**: Tools for analysing data, ranging from essential reporting software to advanced AI and ML capabilities.
- **Security Measures**: Technologies that protect data integrity, prevent unauthorised breaches, and ensure compliance with data protection regulations.

Investing in scalable, user-friendly, and secure technology platforms is essential for your team's long-term success in using data.

Consequences of No or Poor Data Strategy:

Ignoring or neglecting a robust data strategy can lead to significant setbacks. It's like sailing without a map. You might eventually get to your destination, but not without unnecessary detours and wasted efforts.

So, what happens if you don't have a solid data strategy? The consequences can be severe:

- **Missed Opportunities**: Valuable data remains untapped, and you miss chances of innovating.
- **Inefficiencies**: Without standard processes, you face errors and redundancies.
- **Poor Decisions**: Inaccurate or incomplete data leads to misguided strategies.
- **Competitive Disadvantage**: Competitors leveraging data will outpace you.
- **Compliance Risks**: Lack of data governance can lead to legal issues and damage your reputation.

Let's look at some real-world examples.

Case Study: Blockbuster's Collapse: A Data Strategy Failure

Remember Blockbuster? They were once the go-to place for movie rentals. Despite having a wealth of customer data, such as rental histories and preferences, they failed to leverage it to anticipate market trends or personalise customer experiences. They didn't analyse their data to predict the shift toward digital streaming, nor did they use it to offer tailored recommendations. In contrast, Netflix started as a DVD rental service but quickly embraced data analytics. They used customer data to develop personalised recommendation algorithms, predicting what you watch next. Netflix also recognised the growing demand for online streaming and adapted its business model accordingly.

Blockbuster's inability to effectively use its data led to a significant loss of market share. They even had the opportunity to buy Netflix for $50 million in 2000, but dismissed it. By 2010, Blockbuster filed for bankruptcy, closing thousands of stores and laying off countless employees. Meanwhile, Netflix soared to become a global entertainment giant.

Blockbuster's story highlights the importance of having a solid data strategy. They had the data but lacked the vision and strategy to use it effectively. A robust data strategy might've enabled them to pivot and remain competitive. Instead, this oversight cost them their business.

Case Study: The Post Office Horizon Scandal: A Data Strategy Disaster

The Horizon IT scandal in the UK is a stark example of how flawed data systems and poor governance can lead to disastrous outcomes, not just for a company but for individuals' lives.

So, what went wrong?

Around 1999, the Post Office implemented the Horizon IT system to record financial transactions across its branches. However, the system had lots of bugs and errors, leading to accounting discrepancies. Instead of investigating the system flaws, the Post Office relied heavily on this inaccurate data to accuse over 700 sub-postmasters of theft and fraud.

There was a complete lack of data governance and quality management. Sub-postmasters had no transparent way to challenge the data or rectify errors. The company ignored the possibility that the system could be at fault.

The fallout was severe. The flawed Horizon IT system led to the wrongful prosecution of over 700 sub-postmasters, many of whom faced reputational damage, financial ruin, and even imprisonment. As of February 2024, 101 convictions have been overturned, and over £160 million has been paid in compensation across various schemes. The scandal caused severe reputational damage and loss of public trust in both the Post Office and Fujitsu, who developed the IT system. Additionally, Fujitsu reported £50m-£60m in lost potential revenue because of this scandal.

This case highlights the critical need for data quality management and governance. Companies must ensure their data systems are reliable and that there's a transparent process for addressing discrepancies. The human cost of poor data strategy can be devastating, affecting not just organisational performance but lives and livelihoods.

Introducing the Six-Step Data Strategy Framework

There are many data strategy frameworks out there, each with its strengths. In practice, companies blend multiple frameworks to maximise their benefits. Over the years, I've developed a six-step framework that I've found effective. This roadmap will guide you in aligning your data efforts with your business goals, ensuring that your data strategy is practical and impactful.

Step 1: Define Business Objectives and Align Data Initiatives

Before diving into data projects, it's critical to understand what you're trying to achieve. Too often, business stakeholders want solutions that don't address their actual needs. This happens at all levels of the business, from project managers to directors. For example, a project manager might ask for specific KPIs that don't effectively influence their project outcomes. Similarly, a director might want to use AI to make more accurate decisions than their field engineers, but what they actually need is better data infrastructure and quality.

By engaging in dialogue with stakeholders, you can uncover the root causes of their requests and ensure that your data initiatives genuinely align with business objectives. This approach saves time and resources, leading to more effective solutions. It is essential to recognise that business objectives are sometimes different from department objectives. There may be cases where, if one department benefits, another might be negatively affected.

To address these potential conflicts, ask questions that clarify priorities and iron out any discrepancies. This process helps meet the overall business goals without creating internal conflicts.

Once you've clarified the genuine needs and priorities, break down the business objectives into manageable parts. This makes it easier to map specific data initiatives to each business goal, creating a cohesive strategy that addresses the company's priorities.

Step 2: Assess Your Company's Data Landscape

Understanding where you stand is essential for planning where you want to go. Assessing your data maturity gives you a clear picture of your current capabilities and highlights areas for improvement. The key areas to evaluate include:

- **Data Management Practices:** How is data collected, stored, and maintained?
- **Technological Infrastructure:** Do you have the right tools and platforms?
- **People and Skills:** Does your team have the expertise?
- **Cultural Readiness:** Is there a data-driven mindset in the company?

This data maturity model will help you identify strengths to leverage and gaps that need addressing. For instance, you might have advanced analytics tools but need more skilled personnel to use them effectively. Recognising this allows you to prioritise hiring or training initiatives.

Step 3: Grow a Data-Driven Culture

A data strategy is only as effective as the people implementing it. Fostering a data-driven culture ensures that data becomes a critical asset and an integral part of decision-making processes.

Promoting data literacy is essential. Invest in training programs to enhance data literacy across the company. When everyone understands the value of data and feels comfortable using analytical tools, the entire team can contribute to data initiatives.

You also want to encourage collaboration by promoting cross-functional teams and breaking down silos. When teams and departments collaborate, they can share insights and foster innovation.

Leadership commitment is critical since it sets the tone. When executives promote data initiatives and data-driven decision-making, they signal to the entire company that data is a priority.

Step 4: Develop Effective Processes

Processes are the glue that holds your data strategy together. They ensure consistency, quality, and compliance. Implementing data governance involves defining clear policies for data access, usage, and security. This minimises risks like data breaches and ensures compliance with regulators.

You want to create SOPs to standardise existing data practices, which improve efficiency and reliability. This reduces errors and makes it easier for new team members to on-board and get up to speed.

Adopting agile methodologies is crucial. The data landscape is constantly developing. Agile approaches allow you to adapt to changes and incorporate real-time feedback quickly. This is important for AI and ML projects where experimentation and adaptation are key.

Step 5: Empower Your People with the Right Tools and Technology

Having the right tools is essential for unlocking the full potential of your data.

You should choose analytics platforms and technologies that meet your company's needs, are scalable, and align with your technical requirements.

Accessibility is vital. The technologies and tools should be easy to use to encourage widespread adoption. If only a few people can use them, you'll limit the impact of your data initiative.

Lastly, remember to invest in technologies that protect data privacy and comply with relevant regulations. This safeguards your company against legal and reputational risks.

Step 6: Execute and Sustain

With the foundation in place, you want to begin implementing your data initiatives with a focus on sustainability and continuous improvement. Start with pilot projects and initiatives that can show value quickly. Early successes build momentum and support for larger projects.

If you can't measure something, you can't manage it.

Establish KPIs aligned with your business objectives. Regularly monitor progress to identify areas for improvement. Lastly, be prepared to refine your approach based on feedback, emerging technologies, and changing business needs.

Summary

Understanding and implementing a data strategy isn't just a technical endeavour; it's a transformative journey for your company. By focusing on people, mindset, processes, and technology, you can turn data from a passive resource into a strategic asset.

We've seen how companies like Blockbuster suffered from ignoring data trends while others faced severe consequences due to poor data governance. Don't let your company fall into the same traps.

In the chapters ahead, we'll explore how aligning data strategies with your business objectives can take your company to the next level. Together, we'll explore how to turn data from a passive resource into a dynamic catalyst for success.

Chapter 2:
Aligning Data Strategy with Business Objectives

Have you ever invested in data initiatives only to wonder why they're not delivering the expected business results? I've seen this scenario happen in many companies through my engagements and in the news. It's like having a high-performance sports car, but no idea where you're heading. No matter how advanced the vehicle is, you're merely burning fuel and getting nowhere without a clear destination.

In this chapter, we'll explore the first step of the data strategy framework: aligning your data strategy with your business strategy. As previously mentioned, data is not merely a byproduct of operations, but a strategic asset. But its true power is unlocked only when it's aligned with your business objectives. This alignment ensures that your data efforts aren't just technologically impressive but strategically relevant, driving meaningful outcomes that propel your business forward.

Why Aligning Data Strategy with Business Strategy Matters

Imagine pouring resources into state-of-the-art data technologies without clearly understanding how they'll help achieve your business goals. Frustrating. According to a study from Seagate and IDC, the average organisation analyses only about 57% of its data. That means over half the data goes unused, a massive waste of potential and a missed opportunity.

You bridge this gap by aligning your data strategy with your business strategy. You ensure that every data initiative serves a clear purpose and directly contributes to your organization's objectives. In other words, you're not just collecting data for data's sake; you're turning it into actionable insights that drive your business forward.

Understanding Business Strategy

Before diving deeper, let's clarify what business strategy means. Simply put, a business strategy is your organization's game plan for achieving its long-term goals and maintaining a competitive edge. It's about deciding where you want to go and how you'll get there. This strategy operates on three levels: corporate, business unit, and functional.

Corporate-Level Strategy

At the highest level, corporate-level strategy defines your company's overall scope and direction. It answers big-picture questions like: Should we diversify into new industries? Should we consider mergers or acquisitions? For example, a company might expand into renewable energy to promote sustainability and drive long-term growth.

Data Alignment Considerations: At this level, your data strategy should support these broad objectives. If you're entering new markets, your data initiatives might focus on market analysis or assessing customer needs in those regions.

Business-Level Strategy

The business-level strategy zooms in on how each business unit competes in its specific market. It's about positioning your products or services to gain a competitive edge. For instance, a division specializing in cybersecurity software might aim to differentiate itself through cutting-edge technology and exceptional customer support. Overall, the business-level strategy ensures the business unit competes effectively in its market while contributing to the organization's overall objectives.

Data Alignment Considerations: Here, data can help you understand customer preferences, analyse competitors, and optimize your offerings. Use data analytics to tailor products to specific market segments or to identify emerging trends that would give you an advantage.

Functional-Level Strategy

At the operational level, functional strategy involves department-specific plans that support both the business and corporate strategies. This includes areas like marketing, finance, human resources, and operations. For example, your marketing team might develop a digital strategy that leverages social media to increase brand awareness.

Data Alignment Considerations: Data initiatives at this level aim to optimize departmental performance. You might use customer data to create targeted, personalized campaigns in marketing. In operations, data analytics would help streamline processes or improve operational efficiency.

Understanding these business strategy levels allows you to appropriately align your data initiatives across the company. This ensures that your data efforts contribute meaningfully to your corporate goals, competitive positioning, and operational excellence. Next, we'll explore different types of business values, which will help you develop more precise strategies and maximize their overall impact.

Types of Business Value

So, what kinds of value can you expect when your data strategy aligns with your business objectives? Let's explore four key areas:

1. Enhanced Customer Understanding and Experience
2. Smarter Product and Service Decisions
3. Improved Business Processes and Operational Efficiency
4. Boosted Financial Performance

Enhanced Customer Understanding and Experience

In today's customer-centric market, having a deep understanding of your customers is paramount. Data can provide profound insights into customer behaviour, preferences, and needs. We've all seen how Netflix aligned its data with customer-focused objectives, enabling them to create a personalized recommendation system that propelled them to become the top player in the industry.

Case Study: Customer Insight from Tesco's Clubcard

Take Tesco's Clubcard loyalty program. You might remember when loyalty cards were just about collecting points. Tesco took it further by using the Clubcard to gather detailed customer shopping data. They analysed purchasing patterns to tailor promotions and product offerings to individual customers.

This data-driven approach allowed Tesco to develop detailed profiles of their customers' buying behaviours and preferences over time. This provides a more personalized shopping experience and a product range that's better aligned with their customers' needs. By receiving more tailored offers and finding more products that they like, customers' satisfaction and loyalty would increase. The results were impressive. As of early 2024, Tesco Clubcard membership grew to over 16.3 million, and Tesco saw significant increases in sales and profits.

By aligning their data strategy with their goal of enhancing customer experience, Tesco turned data into a powerful tool for growth.

Smarter Product and Service Decisions

Data-driven decision-making empowers you to innovate and improve your products and services effectively. By leveraging data analytics, you can make more informed choices about product development and service offerings and ensure they align closely with market demands and customer expectations.

Case Study: BBC iPlayer's Personalized Recommendation Engine

Let's look at BBC's iPlayer. Similar to the above, by analysing viewing habits and user interactions, BBC has been able to personalize content for its viewers. This has made it easier for users to discover programs they'd enjoy, enhancing their overall experience.

The impact was substantial. In 2024, the users grew by over 20% compared to the previous year. Increased user engagement and satisfaction have helped BBC maintain its position in the increasingly competitive streaming market.

By aligning its data strategy with its objective of improving user experience, BBC made smarter decisions that directly benefited its audience.

Improved Business Processes and Operational Efficiency

Operational efficiency is critical for profitability and competitiveness. Data can help you streamline operations, reduce costs, and improve performance across departments.

Case Study: Network Rail's IoT Sensor Powered Predictive Maintenance

Network Rail, which manages the majority of the UK's railway network, used data to transform its maintenance operations. It installed thousands of sensors on its equipment to collect real-time performance data. By continuously analysing this data, it's shifting from a reactive maintenance regime to a proactive one by predicting and addressing failures before they occur.

I previously led a team developing predictive maintenance models for signalling assets. The impact was remarkable. Network Rail improved safety, reduced maintenance costs, and minimized service disruptions. They received fewer fines by turning data into actionable insights that significantly enhanced operational efficiency.

Boosted Financial Performance

Ultimately, aligning your data strategy with business objectives should positively impact your financial performance. Data-driven strategies can lead to increased revenue and reduced costs.

I was hired to identify strategies to increase customer lifetime value during an old engagement with a coffee shop company. After analysing their shopping data, I discovered that offering promotions at specific early stages can help build habits that encourage long-term customer retention. This approach substantially boosted the clients' lifetime customer value and enabled them to speed up their marketing efforts.

Case Study: Rolls-Royce's Engine Health Management

Rolls-Royce transitioned from merely selling engines to offering comprehensive long-term service agreements, known as 'Total Care.' Under these agreements, airlines pay Rolls-Royce based on the engines' actual hours, while Rolls-Royce provides ongoing maintenance and support services.

By leveraging data from sensors embedded in their engines, Rolls-Royce monitors performance in real-time and predicts maintenance requirements. This proactive, data-driven approach maximizes the engines' asset life, enhances reliability, and ensures higher airline availability.

This strategic shift has created a steady and predictable revenue stream for Rolls-Royce. In 2017, Rolls-Royce's services revenues of £4.2 billion accounted for 53% of its total revenues. It has also reduced operational costs for both Rolls-Royce and its clients by minimizing unexpected downtimes and optimizing maintenance schedules.

Rolls-Royce has successfully innovated its business model by aligning its data initiatives with its financial objectives. This has resulted in substantial revenue growth, with around half of the Rolls-Royce civil engines fleet now covered by long-term service agreements and 80% of new business incorporating long-term support elements.

Alignment Challenges

By now, I hope you're clear that aligning data strategy with business objectives has substantial benefits. However, aligning your data strategy with your business objectives isn't always smooth. Have you ever felt like your data initiatives and business goals are on different wavelengths?

Well, you're not alone.

Many companies struggle with misaligned priorities and a lack of cross-functional understanding. Let's explore the common hurdles that can make synchronizing your business and data strategies seem like an uphill battle.

Misaligned Priorities and Timelines

One of the biggest challenges is that business and data teams often operate on different timelines. Business units might be laser-focused on quarterly targets and immediate market pressures, craving quick wins. Meanwhile, data initiatives typically require longer-term investments and careful planning.

Imagine your marketing team wants instant insights to tweak an ongoing campaign. They turn to the data team, hoping for rapid analysis. However, the data specialists need time to collect, clean, and interpret the relevant information. It's like pairing a sprinter with a marathon runner; they're both athletes but trained at entirely different paces.

This misalignment can lead to frustration on both sides. The business team might feel the data team is too slow, while the data professionals might think the business team doesn't appreciate the complexities involved.

Balancing Short-Term Wins with Long-Term Vision

Similar to the above, there's always a tension between the need for immediate results and long-term strategic goals. Business strategies often demand quick wins to demonstrate value to stakeholders. In contrast, data strategies usually require sustained effort before yielding significant outcomes.

For example, your sales department might push for a rapid deployment of a predictive model to boost this quarter's numbers. Rushing the process could lead to a less accurate model that fails to deliver and potentially erodes trust in data initiatives. It's like choosing between grabbing fast food and preparing a nutritious meal; one satisfies immediate hunger, but the other promotes long-term health.

Lack of a Common Language

Have you ever sat in a meeting where it feels like everyone is talking, but no one is genuinely communicating? That's often the case between business leaders and data professionals. Business leaders struggle to express their needs in technical terms, while data specialists find it challenging to translate complex analytics into actionable business insights.

It's as if both teams are speaking different dialects of the same language. They're in the same conversation, but crucial nuances get lost in translation. This communication gap can cause misunderstandings, duplicated efforts, or missed opportunities.

Evolving Business Landscape vs. Data Infrastructure Rigidity

Your business strategy might need to pivot quickly in response to new opportunities or threats in today's fast-paced market. However, your data infrastructure may need to be more agile to keep up.

Suppose you decide to enter a new market or launch a groundbreaking product. Your existing data systems might need to be equipped to provide the insights you need about this uncharted territory. It's akin to trying to steer a large ship; turning takes time. The business can change direction swiftly, but the data infrastructure needs to catch up, creating a disconnect.

Overcoming the Alignment Challenges

So, how do you bridge these gaps and create harmony between your business and data strategies? Here are some approaches that I've seen work effectively:

Foster Data Literacy Across the Company

Encourage your business leaders to develop a basic understanding of data concepts. Likewise, help your data professionals grasp key business principles. Communication improves dramatically when everyone has at least a foundational knowledge of each other's domains.

Create Cross-Functional Teams

Form teams that include both business and data professionals working towards common goals. This collaboration fosters mutual understanding and ensures data initiatives are directly aligned with business needs.

Develop Flexible Data Architecture

Invest in adaptable data systems that can develop with your changing business landscape. This might mean adopting scalable cloud solutions or modular technologies that allow for quick adjustments.

Establish Clear Governance

Define roles, responsibilities, and decision-making processes that involve stakeholders from both the business and data sides. Clear governance structures help prevent misalignment and ensure accountability.

Implement Agile Methodologies

Adopt agile practices that allow for iterative progress and regular reassessment of priorities. This approach enables your teams to deliver incremental value while staying responsive to changing needs.

By proactively addressing these challenges, you can transform potential friction points into opportunities for collaboration and innovation. Remember, the goal isn't to make your data strategy subservient to your business strategy, and vice versa. It's about creating a shared vision where both strategies work in concert to drive your company forward. We'll dive deeper into these approaches in later chapters of this book.

Defining Business Objectives and Aligning with Data Strategy

Now that we've explored different types of business objectives, as well as the benefits and challenges of aligning business with data strategies, let's talk about how to implement them. It begins with a deep understanding of what your company aims to achieve and how data can help you achieve it. This isn't just a checkbox exercise; it's about introspection and asking the right questions to uncover where data can make the most significant impact.

Here are some questions I often ask when I join a new engagement:

1. What Are Our Top Strategic Objectives That Could Benefit from Data and AI Implementation?

Start by identifying your primary goals. Are you looking to expand into new markets, boost customer retention, or enhance operational efficiency? Once you've pinpointed these objectives, think about how data initiatives can support them. For example, if customer retention is a priority, could data analytics help you understand customer behaviour better to tailor your services?

2. What Obstacles Are Impeding Progress Toward Our Data-Driven Goals?

Be honest about the challenges you're facing. Do you have data silos that prevent a unified view of information? Is outdated technology holding you back? There may be a skills gap within your team. Recognizing these obstacles is the first step toward developing strategies to overcome them.

3. What Data Privacy and Security Challenges Do We Face?

Data privacy and security are more critical than ever in today's world. Are you compliant with regulations like GDPR or CCPA? Understanding your legal obligations is essential. Implementing robust data governance protects sensitive information and builds trust with your customers.

4. How Much Time and Resources Are Allocated to Integrating Tools and Systems?

Take a close look at your current data infrastructure. Are you spending excessive time and resources piecing together disparate tools and systems? If so, it might be worth investing in integration platforms or unified systems. Streamlining your tech stack can free up resources and improve efficiency.

5. What Key Data Capabilities Are Missing?

Identify any gaps in your data capabilities. Do you need advanced analytics, artificial intelligence, or real-time data processing? Knowing what's missing allows you to plan for acquiring or developing these capabilities, whether through hiring new talent, training existing staff, or partnering with external experts.

6. What Metrics and KPIs Do We Use to Evaluate Success?

Establish clear metrics aligned with your business objectives. What does success look like for your company? By defining key performance indicators (KPIs), you can make informed decisions, monitor progress, and adjust your strategies as needed.

By thoughtfully considering these questions, you're not just aligning your data initiatives with your business objectives; you're laying the groundwork for meaningful, data-driven success. Remember, the goal is to turn data from a passive asset into an active catalyst for growth and innovation.

Summary

Aligning your data strategy with your business objectives isn't a one-time exercise; it's an ongoing commitment. It requires clear objectives, open communication, and a willingness to adapt.

By understanding the different levels of business strategy and the types of value that data alignment can generate, you can more effectively integrate data initiatives into your overall planning. Addressing challenges head-on and asking the right questions enables you to identify opportunities where data can have the most significant impact.

In today's data-driven world, organizations that successfully align their data and business strategies are better positioned to innovate, compete, and thrive. By making data a central component of your strategic planning, you transform it from a mere operational necessity into a powerful driver of growth and sustained success.

In the next chapter, we'll explore the data maturity model. This will help you understand your current state regarding your data capabilities and guide you toward data-driven excellence.

Chapter 3:
Assessing Your Data Maturity

Before you can leverage data strategically to accelerate growth and innovation, it's crucial to understand where your company currently stands. Have you ever tried to improve something before assessing its current state? It's like setting out on a journey without a map; you might eventually get somewhere, but probably not where you intended. In Chapter 1, we introduced the data strategy framework, and this chapter will focus on the second step: assessing your organization's current state in data maturity.

Understanding your data capabilities isn't just beneficial - it's essential. A data maturity model is a growth chart for your company's data journey. It outlines the stages of evolution from basic data collection to advanced analytics that drive decision-making and open new business opportunities. Knowing where your company stands in the model allows you to identify gaps, prioritize initiatives, and see how you stack up against industry standards or your competitors.

Several frameworks exist to help companies assess their data maturity. For instance, Dell's Data Maturity Model uses a four-star system ranging from 'Data Aware' to 'Data-Driven.' Gartner has a similar model with five levels, from 'Basic' to 'Transformational', focusing on how data influences decision-making processes. While each model has its nuances, they all share the goal of helping you understand and improve your data capabilities.

Drawing from these frameworks and my own consulting experience, I've developed a five-step data maturity model centred around the four key components discussed in Chapter 1: mindset, people, process, and tools/technology. Let's dive into what each stage looks like, starting with the first step, the Emerging Stage.

Step 1: The Emerging Stage

At the Emerging Stage, businesses are just beginning their data journey. The data practices in these companies are unstructured and reactive, with a limited awareness of the data's strategic value. Data management is often fragmented and inconsistent, making it challenging to leverage your data assets effectively.

Characteristics

Mindset

The culture around data at this stage is lacking. There's little emphasis on data-driven decision-making. Employees may not have the skills to interpret or use data effectively, and the value of data isn't widely recognized throughout the company. I've seen companies where data is collected but then sit unused for decades, like books gathering dust on a shelf. Does that sound familiar?

Senior leadership might not prioritize data initiatives or see data as a strategic asset. Decisions are often made based on intuition or experiences rather than hard data. Without executive support, it's tough to push data projects forward. This gap in data literacy and leadership focus can hold your company back from gaining a competitive edge using data.

People

In this stage, specialized data roles like analysts or data scientists are often missing. Employees might have limited data management or analysis skills, and there's usually no formal training to help them grow in this area. As a graduate, I worked with clients where data responsibilities were added onto someone's already full plate with no extra support or resources. Let's just say progress wasn't fast there.

Data roles and responsibilities are often undefined or assigned informally, leading to confusion and inefficiency. Without a dedicated data team or a Chief Data Officer (CDO), data management lacks proper oversight and strategic direction.

Process

When it comes to processes, data governance is often missing in action. There might be little to no data policies or standards, or they're applied inconsistently. Data management tends to be ad hoc and reactive. Very often, you'll see different departments in an company handle data differently, which creates silos and hinders collaboration.

Data quality can be a significant headache. Issues with accuracy, completeness, and consistency are common. Without standardized data cleansing or validation processes, problems are often addressed only when they cause a crisis, making it hard to trust any insights you get from your data.

Tools and Technology

At this stage, your technological landscape may consist of siloed data systems that don't communicate with each other. Outdated infrastructure can limit your ability to collect and analyse data effectively. Without a centralized data repository or warehouse, integrating and accessing data becomes a real challenge. Think of scattered Excel spreadsheets on different employees' laptops, making it difficult to consolidate information.

Advanced analytical tools are absent or underutilized. Decision-making rarely relies on data insights, and reporting is often a manual, time-consuming process. Without the right tools, extracting meaningful insights to drive business value is challenging.

Common Challenges

Organizations at the Emerging Stage often face significant hurdles that impede their ability to leverage data effectively:

- **Lack of Data Strategy and Vision**: Without a clear direction, data initiatives become fragmented and often ineffective. There's no overarching plan to guide efforts, leading to wasted resources and missed opportunities. Early in my career, I've seen and worked on isolated data projects that don't seem to align with broader business goals. Does that ring a bell?
- **Poor Data Quality**: Inconsistent data management leads to unreliable information, affecting decision-making. Data inaccuracies can erode trust among stakeholders and hinder operational efficiency. It's like trying to build a house on a shaky foundation.

- **Minimal Data Literacy**: Limited awareness and understanding of data across the company results in the underutilization of available information. Employees might not realise how data can enhance their roles, leading to resistance or apathy toward data initiatives.
- **Siloed Data Systems**: Disconnected systems prevent a holistic view, making comprehensive analysis difficult. This fragmentation hinders collaboration and stops the company from gaining insights that span multiple departments.
- **Resource Constraints**: Limited budget allocation for data initiatives due to undervaluing data's potential impact. Without adequate funding, investing in the necessary tools, training, or personnel to advance data capabilities is challenging.

Typical Data initiatives

At this stage, data initiatives are limited and reactive. You might collect data to meet immediate business needs or comply with regulations. Reporting often involves manual data extraction and spreadsheet analysis. These processes are time-consuming and prone to error, limiting their effectiveness.

There may be isolated attempts at data cleansing or company, but these are one-off projects rather than part of an ongoing process. Without a strategic approach, these efforts fail to produce lasting improvements or significantly advance your data maturity.

Let's take a family-owned bakery in a small town as an example. Companies in this stage might use basic spreadsheets to track daily sales and inventory. However, decisions about what to bake are still based on the owner's intuition and experience rather than the data that they've collected. Also, the data collected is inconsistent, and there's no formal process for using data to improve their operations.

Transition Indicators

Despite the challenges, certain signs suggest you're ready to progress to the next stage of data maturity:

- **Leadership Awareness**: Increased recognition of data's potential value among senior management. Leaders begin to understand that data can drive strategic decision-making and offer a competitive edge.
- **Standardization Efforts**: Initial attempts to standardize data collection and storage practices emerge. This might involve implementing basic data entry protocols or consolidating data sources.
- **Growing Demand for Insights**: Departments are starting to request data-driven insights to inform decisions. As teams recognize the benefits, they seek out information to enhance their performance.
- **Role Definition**: The need for dedicated data roles or responsibilities is recognized. You may consider hiring data professionals or assigning data stewardship duties to existing staff.
- **Quality Initiatives**: Preliminary efforts to address data quality issues are underway. This could include basic data cleansing projects or establishing simple validation checks.
- **Exploration of Tools**: Interest in adopting more advanced analytic tools or platforms surfaces. Your company starts evaluating software solutions to improve data analysis and reporting capabilities.

These indicators reflect a shift in mindset and a growing appreciation for data's strategic importance. They signal readiness to invest in the foundational elements necessary to advance their data maturity.

Benefits and Limitations

Operating at the Emerging Stage comes with simplicity and low overhead. You can function without significant investment in data infrastructure or specialized skills. However, this stage has notable limitations. The lack of structured data management leads to inefficiencies and missed opportunities. Decision-making is often based on incomplete or inaccurate information, making it hard to trust your choices.

Moving beyond this stage allows you to start leveraging data more effectively, improving decision-making and operational efficiency. However, progress requires a shift in mindset, investment in skills and technology, and a commitment to developing more mature data practices.

Key Focus Areas for Improvement

To move beyond the Emerging Stage, focus on these critical areas:

- **Establish Basic Data Governance Policies:** Create foundational policies for data ownership, entry standards, storage, and security. Clear guidelines help employees manage data consistently, reducing errors and improving quality. Companies often transform their data practices by implementing straightforward policies. Start in business units where it'll have the highest business impact and success rate.
- **Increase Awareness of Data-Driven Decision-Making:** Shift the culture to value data by hosting workshops, sharing success stories, and integrating data discussions into meetings. When employees see the benefits of data-driven strategies, they're more likely to support these initiatives. Remember, change starts with awareness.
- **Build Foundational Data Skills Through Targeted Training:** Bridge skills gaps by offering data analysis,

visualization, and management best practices courses. Enhancing data literacy enables employees to contribute meaningfully to data initiatives. What training would benefit your team the most?

- **Integrate Data Systems to Reduce Silos:** Very often, you'll see different departments in an company handle data differently, creating data silos, basically isolated data systems that hinder collaboration. You want to break down data silos, implement integration tools, consolidate databases, and standardize data formats. This fosters better collaboration and comprehensive analysis. Integrating key systems can lead to significant insights and efficiencies. If your company hasn't done this yet, this could be a game-changer for you.

Focusing on these areas will help businesses lay the groundwork for more mature data and analytics practices. It's about moving toward a more structured and strategic approach to data management that positions your company to harness data as a true strategic asset.

Step 2: The Empowered Stage

Moving forward on your data journey, the Empowered Stage is where companies begin to recognize the value of data and analytics. Have you ever noticed teams in your company starting to ask for data to back up their decisions? This is a sign that you're transitioning into a more data-aware culture. However, efforts at this stage are often fragmented, lacking a cohesive strategy that ties everything together.

Characteristics

Mindset

At this point, there's a growing acknowledgment across the company that data matters. Some employees are starting to understand the potential of data-driven decision-making. While dashboards and analytical tools are being developed, there isn't sufficient training, established processes, or ongoing support to ensure they're used effectively. As a result, several of these tools end up sitting on the shelves again. Does that resonate with you?

Senior leaders are beginning to support data initiatives, but the commitment isn't yet organisation-wide. Decisions may sometimes be based on data, especially for high-profile projects, but intuition and past experience still play a significant role. It's like having one foot on the gas and one on the brake. You make progress, but it's slower than it could be.

People

Specialized data roles start to emerge at this stage. You might have a data analyst or a business intelligence specialist on board. However, these roles are often siloed within specific departments. Even in 2023, I've seen entire regulatory teams relying on basic spreadsheets and VBA that frequently break while the rest of the business boasts several advanced analytics and data science teams.

Skills gaps become apparent. While some teams have the expertise to handle data effectively, others are left behind. Formal training programs are sporadic or limited in scope, leading to an uneven distribution of data literacy across the business.

Process

When it comes to processes, initial data governance policies and standards are introduced. These are often focused on immediate concerns like data access and security. Data management practices have become more consistent but aren't fully standardized yet. You might notice that one department has a solid data entry process while another still uses ad hoc methods.

Efforts to improve data quality are underway. Basic data cleansing and validation procedures are implemented, usually in response to specific issues that have cropped up. For example, an Excel report might have highlighted discrepancies in customer data, prompting a clean-up initiative. While these efforts are a step in the right direction, they're often reactive rather than proactive.

Tools and Technology

At this stage, companies begin integrating data systems, reducing some of the silos that previously existed. You might adopt more modern data technologies like a basic data warehouse or simple analytics platforms. However, these tools are often implemented to meet specific project needs rather than as a unified strategy.

Basic business intelligence (BI) tools are rolled out, enabling some level of data analysis and reporting. Teams start creating dashboards and generating reports, but without standardized data definitions, these can vary between departments. In most of my engagements, different data sources and teams have different figures for the same metrics, causing confusion and mistrust in the data.

Common Challenges

Organizations at the Empowered Stage often face significant hurdles that impede their ability to leverage data effectively:

- **Lack of Unified Data Strategy**: Without a cohesive plan, data initiatives remain fragmented and often duplicate efforts. There are companies where multiple departments purchased similar analytics tools independently, and sometimes even the same one, hiking contract prices.
- **Limited Resources and Expertise**: Dedicated resources for data initiatives are scarce, making it hard to scale projects. Data

professionals may be overburdened, leading to burnout and turnover.

- **Inconsistent Data Governance**: Policies exist but aren't uniformly applied across the company, leading to discrepancies and compliance risks. This inconsistency can erode trust in the data and the decisions based on it.
- **Resistance to Change**: Employees accustomed to ad hoc processes may resist new data practices. Change management becomes a critical issue to address.
- **Demonstrating Value**: Proving the ROI of data initiatives to secure further investment can be challenging. Without clear metrics, it's tough to justify additional resources.

Typical Data Initiatives

At this stage, companies typically engage in projects that address immediate needs or low-hanging fruit. Implementing basic data quality checks and cleansing processes becomes a priority to improve the reliability of existing data. By focusing on data validation and correction, you enhance the accuracy of your data, which supports better decision-making.

Piloting departmental analytics projects is another common initiative. These projects show the value of data-driven decision-making within specific areas, providing tangible results that can be showcased to stakeholders. Success in these pilots often builds momentum for broader data initiatives across the organisation.

Establishing data governance committees or working groups helps formalize data management practices. These groups develop initial policies and standards, addressing issues like data access, security, and quality. While still in the early stages, this formalization lays the groundwork for more comprehensive governance structures in the future.

Conducting data literacy workshops for key stakeholders is also typical. These workshops aim to build awareness and skills across the company, empowering employees to utilize data more effectively within their roles. Enhancing data literacy contributes to fostering a culture that values and leverages data.

Case Study: Nemours Children's Data Literacy Initiative

The above is exactly what Nemours Children's Health System did. Although the company holds a vast amount of health records, the workforce struggled to leverage this data effectively. To address this challenge, Nemours implemented 'Data Swagger Sessions' to improve data literacy across the business. They also created actionable dashboards tailored to various departments, appointed 'citizen developers' to support data governance, and focused on making data more accessible and understandable.

These efforts led to tangible improvements. Frontline staff began each day with patient-first metrics, ensuring patient care remained the top priority. Planning processes were enhanced through the use of standardized metrics, resulting in better coordination and efficiency. Additionally, employee empowerment in data usage increased, allowing staff to make more informed, data-driven decisions. These initiatives significantly enhanced patient experience and care delivery, strengthening Nemours' service offerings within the healthcare sector.

Transition Indicators

Several signs indicate that an organisation is moving from the Empowered Stage to the next level of data maturity:

- **Growing Demand for Data-Driven Insights**: Departments increasingly request data analyses to support their decision-making processes. This heightened interest shows a shift toward valuing data as a critical asset, leading to more frequent collaboration and utilization of analytical tools.

- **Increased Executive Support for Data Initiatives**: Senior leadership begins allocating specific budgets and resources for data projects. This investment demonstrates a commitment to integrating data into strategic objectives, accelerating the adoption of data practices organisation-wide.

- **Emergence of Data Champions Across Business Units**: Key individuals within various departments start advocating for data-driven approaches. These data champions promote the benefits of using data in daily operations, influence others, and foster a data-centric culture within their teams.

- **Rise in Cross-Functional Collaboration on Data Projects**: Teams from different departments work together on data initiatives, breaking down organizational silos. This collaboration enhances knowledge sharing and leads to more comprehensive insights that benefit the entire organisation.

- **More Consistent Application of Data Governance Practices**: Basic data governance policies are applied more uniformly across the business. Consistency in data handling improves data quality and builds trust in the data used for decision-making processes.

- **Recognition of the Need for a Comprehensive Data Strategy**: There is a growing understanding that a unified data strategy is essential for sustained growth and competitiveness. This recognition prompts discussions about long-term planning and aligning data initiatives with the overall business objectives.

- **Allocation of Dedicated Resources for Data Management**: Companies start assigning specific personnel and tools dedicated to managing data assets. Dedicated resources enable more focused and effective data initiatives, enhancing overall data capabilities.

- **Increased Focus on Data Quality and Standardization**: Efforts to improve data accuracy, consistency, and completeness

become a priority. Standardizing data definitions and formats across departments reduces errors and enhances the reliability of insights drawn from the data.
- **Growing Interest in Advanced Analytics Capabilities**: There is increasing curiosity about leveraging advanced analytics techniques like predictive modelling and machine learning. Exploring these capabilities allows businesses to gain deeper insights and gain competitive advantages.
- **Development of Metrics to Measure Data Initiative Impact**: Organizations begin establishing key performance indicators (KPIs) to assess the effectiveness of data projects. Measuring impact helps show the value of data initiatives and guides future investments and strategies.

Benefits and Limitations

The Empowered Stage brings several benefits. Organizations start to see tangible results from their data initiatives, such as improved decision-making in specific areas and increased efficiency in data-related processes. The growing awareness of data's value lays the groundwork for future, more comprehensive strategies. Quick wins can build momentum and support for further investments.

However, this stage also has limitations. The lack of a unified data strategy results in inconsistent practices across departments. Data quality issues may persist due to the absence of standardized processes. The sporadic nature of initiatives can lead to missed opportunities for leveraging data more broadly. While progress is made, the full potential of data-driven decision-making remains largely untapped.

Key Focus Areas for Improvement

To move beyond the Empowered Stage, focus on these critical areas:

- **Developing a Cohesive Data Strategy Aligned with Business Objectives**: Creating a unified data strategy ensures that all data initiatives support your organization's goals. This alignment helps prioritize projects that deliver the most value and provides a roadmap for effectively scaling data capabilities.
- **Expanding Data Governance Frameworks for Consistency**: Enhancing data governance policies and procedures promotes uniformity in data handling across the company. Consistent practices improve data quality, compliance with regulations, and trust in data-driven decisions.
- **Investing in Training Programs to Enhance Data Literacy**: Providing comprehensive training improves employees' ability to work with data effectively. Enhanced data literacy empowers teams to make informed decisions and fosters a data-driven culture throughout the company.
- **Leveraging Business Intelligence Tools Systematically**: Implementing BI tools across departments with standardized data definitions ensures consistent reporting and analysis. Systematic use of these tools enables better decision-making through accessible and reliable insights.
- **Establishing Metrics to Measure the Impact of Data Initiatives**: Developing KPIs helps show the value of data projects for stakeholders. Measuring impact facilitates informed decision-making about future investments and data-related strategic directions.

Overall, being in the Empowered Stage is a significant milestone. It shows that the company recognizes the importance of data, even if it's still figuring out how to harness it fully. Becoming a data-driven company is a journey, not a destination. The key is to keep moving forward, learning, and adapting along the way.

Step 3: The Integrated Stage

By now, you've laid a solid foundation in your data journey. You've moved past the basics and are starting to see the real impact of data on your business. Welcome to The Integrated Stage. In this stage, organizations have established robust data governance frameworks and proactively manage data quality. Data management approaches are more structured and data strategically leveraged across the organisation. This stage marks a significant shift towards a data-driven culture and operational model.

Characteristics

Mindset

At this stage, data-driven decision-making becomes the norm rather than the exception. Your organisation embraces a culture where data is at the heart of every strategy. Employees across all levels understand the value of data and are more comfortable interpreting and using it in their daily tasks. Comprehensive training programs enhance data literacy, making data a shared language within your company.

Leadership doesn't just support data initiatives; they champion them. Executives actively participate in data governance committees and set a top-down example. They recognize data as a strategic asset aligned with business goals. This commitment from the top reinforces the importance of data throughout the organisation.

People

Your team now includes dedicated data professionals, like data stewards and analysts. Cross-functional teams collaborate on data projects, combining domain expertise with technical skills. This collaboration drives innovation and efficiency. Continuous learning is a priority, ensuring your team's skills stay current in a rapidly evolving field.

Clear roles and responsibilities mean there's accountability for data management and utilization. Perhaps you've appointed a Chief Data Officer or similar role to oversee your data strategy. Data stewardship programs are in place to maintain data quality and consistency across departments.

Process

Data governance is no longer an afterthought; it's a well-oiled machine. You have well-defined policies and standards that are consistently enforced. Regular audits and assessments ensure compliance, and data governance committees oversee implementation. Data management processes are standardized and applied uniformly across the organisation.

Data quality isn't just maintained; it's actively monitored and improved. Automated processes handle data cleansing and validation. At this stage, organizations regularly report on data quality metrics and use these insights for continuous improvement. Data quality becomes a shared responsibility, not just the domain of the IT department.

Tools and Technology

At this stage, your technological landscape is now integrated and efficient. Systems communicate seamlessly, facilitating smooth data flow across the organisation. You've likely implemented data lakes or enterprise data warehouses to centralize your data assets. Your infrastructure supports advanced data collection and storage needs, handling increasing data volumes without a hitch.

Advanced analytics and business intelligence tools are widely used. You're not just looking at what happened; you're predicting what will happen. Self-service analytics empower business users to perform their own analyses, democratizing data access. The focus shifts from merely understanding the past to anticipating the future, providing more value to the business.

Common Challenges

Even at the Integrated Stage, organizations face several challenges:

- **Potential Rigidity in Processes**: With established data governance and management processes, you might find it harder to adapt quickly to new data sources or emerging technologies. I've seen clients struggle to incorporate innovative tools because their existing systems were too rigid. This lack of agility can hinder your ability to respond to market changes.
- **Scaling Advanced Analytics**: Expanding sophisticated analytics capabilities across all areas isn't always smooth sailing. Some departments may lag in adoption due to varying levels of data maturity or resistance to change. This inconsistency can prevent the organisation from reaping the full benefits of advanced analytics.
- **Integration of New Technologies**: Introducing new data sources or technologies can pose difficulties, especially if legacy systems are still in place. The complexity of integrating modern tools with older infrastructure can lead to delays and increased costs, slowing down innovation.
- **Ongoing Cultural Shift**: While data-driven decision-making is more common, some individuals may still rely on intuition over data. Continual efforts are needed to promote a data-centric mindset throughout the organisation. Changing long-held habits isn't easy, but it's necessary for progress.
- **Balancing Governance with Flexibility**: Strict data policies might stifle innovation if not managed carefully. It's a challenge to maintain strong governance while allowing flexibility for creative data use. Finding the right balance is crucial to

encourage experimentation without compromising data integrity.

Typical Data Initiatives

At the Integrated Stage, data projects become more sophisticated and strategic. Organizations implement master data management (MDM) programs to ensure data consistency, creating a single source of truth that eliminates discrepancies and enhances decision-making accuracy. This centralized approach reduces confusion and fosters collaboration across departments.

Developing data catalogues is also a priority, as they improve data discovery and usability. Companies often see a boost in productivity when employees can easily find relevant data assets. Additionally, piloting advanced analytics projects, such as predictive modelling, provides valuable insights and demonstrates the tangible benefits of analytics to stakeholders. For instance, organizations have successfully reduced inventory costs by accurately anticipating demand through predictive analytics.

Establishing data quality programs and enhancing data governance frameworks are crucial at this stage. Implementing data quality scorecards ensures data remains accurate and trustworthy, while comprehensive governance policies guide responsible data management. These initiatives build confidence in data-driven strategies and cultivate a culture of accountability and transparency within the organisation.

Case Study: Coca-Cola's Master Data Management Initiative

Here's an example. Coca-Cola struggled with data management and accessibility, making it hard to keep data up-to-date to generate useful insights. Their inventory and delivery analytics were updated only once daily, limiting accurate and timely operational decisions.

To solve this, Coca-Cola migrated their infrastructure to AWS in 2020. They built a data lake on AWS, consolidating 95% of their data from various business areas and developing custom applications to manage inventory, distribution, and delivery. This centralized approach made data more accessible and streamlined their processes.

The results were impressive: analytics team productivity increased by 80%, and key metrics like order fill rate, out-of-stock rate, and orders not received improved by 0.3% to 1%. By adopting AI and machine learning, Coca-Cola enabled more data-driven decisions and streamlined business practices. This transformation allowed them to double their product range, boosting customer satisfaction and revenue. It's a great example of how strategic data initiatives can drive significant business improvements.

Transition Indicators

Recognizing when you're ready to move to the next stage is essential for continued growth. So, how do you know you're prepared to go further, beyond the Integrated Stage?

- **Consistent Use of Advanced Analytics**: Advanced analytics techniques have become standard practice across multiple business functions. Departments regularly use predictive models and complex analyses to inform their decisions, showing a deep integration of these tools into daily operations. This widespread adoption shows a high level of data sophistication.
- **High Level of Data Literacy**: Employees understand and actively use data in their roles. They feel confident interpreting data insights and applying them to their work. Training programs have effectively raised the baseline of data knowledge, enabling more nuanced and strategic use of information.

- **Mature Data Governance Practices**: Your data governance policies are not just documented - they're lived. Practices are consistently followed and regularly reviewed. There's a proactive approach to governance, with adjustments made as needed to accommodate new challenges or opportunities. This maturity ensures that data practices remain aligned with business goals.
- **Seamless Integration of Systems**: Data flows effortlessly across the organisation. Systems are well-integrated, reducing bottlenecks and facilitating real-time access to information. This seamless integration supports more dynamic and responsive decision-making, allowing the organisation to act quickly on insights.
- **Strong Data-Driven Culture**: Leadership consistently relies on data insights for strategic planning. Decisions at all levels are backed by data, and there's organizational pride in being data-driven. This cultural shift permeates every aspect of the business, fostering innovation and continuous improvement.
- **Agile Data Strategies**: Your organisation can quickly adapt data approaches to changing business needs or market conditions. Your data processes are flexible, allowing you to pivot when necessary without significant disruption. This agility indicates you're ready to tackle even more advanced data challenges.

Benefits and Limitations

Reaching the Integrated Stage brings significant benefits, including improved decision-making capabilities and operational efficiency. Data-driven insights lead to more accurate and timely choices, while standardized data management processes streamline workflows and reduce redundancies. This focus on data quality boosts confidence in analytics and reporting, making them more reliable and actionable.

Your organisation gains a competitive edge at this stage by effectively harnessing data. By developing a holistic view of their operations, customer behaviours, and market trends, they can identify and capitalize on opportunities more swiftly than fewer data-mature competitors. Alignment between data initiatives and business objectives ensures that all data-driven efforts directly contribute to the company's strategic goals, driving the business forward.

However, there are limitations to consider. Established data processes can introduce rigidity, making it challenging to adapt quickly to new data sources or emerging technologies. This rigidity may hinder innovation and responsiveness to market changes. Additionally, integrating new technologies with legacy systems can be complex and costly, potentially delaying progress. Balancing strong data governance with the need for flexibility remains an ongoing challenge, as overly strict policies can impede organisation-wide creativity and agility.

Key Focus Areas for Improvement

To move beyond the Integrated Stage, it's essential to focus on key areas that will propel your company forward. Building on your strengths while addressing current limitations will allow even greater data maturity.

- **Enhance Agility in Data Processes**: Find ways to make your data management adaptable to change. This might involve adopting more flexible technologies or revising governance policies for quicker adjustments. Embracing agile methodologies can help your teams respond more effectively to new opportunities.
- **Scale Advanced Analytics**: Invest in training and resources to expand sophisticated analytics capabilities across all departments. Encouraging knowledge sharing between teams can also help. By democratizing advanced analytics, you empower more employees to contribute to innovation.

- **Integrate New Technologies Smoothly**: Develop strategies for incorporating new tools and data sources without disrupting existing systems. This might include adopting modular technologies or using APIs for better compatibility. Planning for scalability and integration from the outset can ease transitions.
- **Continue Cultural Development**: Keep promoting a data-driven mindset at all levels. Share success stories and encourage leaders to model data-centric behaviours. Reinforcing the value of data helps maintain momentum and fosters an environment where data is integral to every decision.
- **Balance Governance with Innovation**: Ensure your data policies support, rather than hinder, innovation. Regularly review governance frameworks to remove unnecessary constraints. By finding the right balance, you can protect data integrity while allowing creativity and experimentation.

You can chart a clear path forward by understanding where you stand in the data maturity model. The Integrated Stage is a significant milestone, but there's always room to grow. Focusing on these key areas will help you leverage your integrated data environment to drive transformative change across your company.

Step 4: The Strategic Stage

When your company reaches the Strategic Stage, data isn't just a resource; it's fully ingrained in every part of your business strategy. it's ingrained in every facet of your business strategy. Have you ever wondered what it would look like if data drove decisions and innovation across your company? At this stage, that's exactly what's happening. Data-driven decision-making is embedded at all levels, and advanced analytics and business intelligence are part of your daily operations.

Characteristics

Mindset

A strong data culture permeates the organisation. Everyone from the frontline staff to senior executives embraces data-informed decision-making. Ongoing training programs ensure high levels of data literacy across all departments. Employees are encouraged to challenge assumptions and use data to drive innovation. Not quite at the Strategic Stage yet, but I remember working with a client whose team meetings always began with reviewing data insights from a KPI dashboard before moving to agenda items. It's a major shift in mentality.

Leadership doesn't just support data initiatives; they champion them. Data is central to organizational strategy and operations. Executives consistently use analytics to inform strategic planning and resource allocation. They set the tone, clarifying that data isn't just a tool but a strategic asset.

People

At this stage, your workforce is highly skilled in data management, analytics, and even data science. Specialized roles like Chief Data Officers are common and crucial in shaping the data landscape. Cross-functional teams tackle complex data challenges, fostering collaboration and knowledge sharing.

Robust governance structures support data initiatives. Roles and responsibilities are clearly defined, ensuring effective collaboration between data teams and other departments. Data stewardship programs are well-established, promoting a shared responsibility for data assets and maintaining high data quality across the organisation.

Process

Comprehensive data governance frameworks ensure data is managed consistently and responsibly. Policies are regularly reviewed and updated to meet evolving needs and regulatory requirements. Data lineage and metadata management practices are in place, clarifying data sources, transformations, and usage. This transparency builds trust and enables more effective data utilization.

High standards of data quality are maintained through continuous monitoring and improvement processes. Automated quality checks and validation procedures are implemented across data pipelines. When issues arise, root cause analyses are conducted to address problems systematically. This proactive approach ensures that your data remains reliable and valuable.

Tools and Technology

Your technological infrastructure is scalable and flexible, supporting growing data demands and diverse use cases. Modern data technologies, including cloud-based solutions, are fully integrated into your IT ecosystem. Real-time data processing capabilities enable timely insights and decision-making. Dashboards update in real-time, allowing managers to make instant decisions and adjustments.

Advanced analytics, including predictive and prescriptive models, are routinely used to inform strategic decisions. Data visualization tools effectively convey insights to stakeholders, promoting data-driven discussions. Self-service analytics platforms empower business users to explore data independently, reducing reliance on IT for routine analysis.

Common Challenges

Even at this advanced stage, challenges persist. While data is deeply integrated into your operations, new complexities emerge that require careful navigation. Recognizing these hurdles to maintain momentum and continue advancing to unlock more business value is essential. Let's explore some of the common challenges organizations face in the Strategic Stage:

- **Managing Complexity**: Implementing sophisticated analytics initiatives while ensuring scalability can be daunting. Balancing cutting-edge models with practical deployment across various business units requires careful planning.
- **Maintaining Strategic Focus**: Keeping data as a strategic priority amidst changing business landscapes and competing initiatives can take time and effort. It's essential to advocate for data-driven decision-making continually.
- **Updating Governance Frameworks**: As new data sources and technologies emerge, governance practices need constant refinement to remain effective.
- **Ethical Concerns**: Leveraging advanced analytics and AI brings ethical considerations around data privacy and security. Navigating these responsibly is crucial.
- **Sustaining Competitive Advantage**: Continuous investment in emerging technologies and methodologies is necessary to stay ahead in the ever-evolving data landscape.

Typical Data Initiatives

Organizations at the Strategic Stage engage in sophisticated data projects that drive innovation and open up new business opportunities. One common initiative is enterprise-wide data integration, where companies implement data lakes or data fabrics to consolidate information from various sources. This unified approach supports diverse analytics use cases, allowing for more comprehensive insights and fostering collaboration across departments.

Another significant focus is on advanced AI and machine learning. Organizations develop complex models to enhance predictive capabilities and automate decision-making processes. For example, machine learning algorithms can forecast market trends or customer behaviour, enabling proactive strategies. Data monetization is also key, with companies creating data products or services that generate additional revenue streams, such as offering analytics services to clients or developing platforms that leverage proprietary data. Establishing data ethics frameworks becomes essential to ensure data is used ethically and complies with regulatory standards, building trust with customers and stakeholders.

Case Study: Network Rail's Predictive Maintenance Initiative

Over the past five years, Network Rail, the UK's largest rail infrastructure company, has implemented several predictive modelling initiatives to transition from a reactive to a proactive maintenance regime. I led multiple projects focused on developing failure prediction capabilities for signalling assets. Utilizing machine learning algorithms, the team analysed live IoT sensor data and other sources to create models that predict potential signalling failures. This provided maintenance teams with more advance warnings to address issues before they caused disruptions, aligning with Network Rail's broader 'predict and prevent' strategy, exemplified by their 'Insight' web application.

Implementing this predictive maintenance system reduced signal failures significantly, enhancing passenger experience by minimizing unexpected delays and service disruptions. This success demonstrated the tangible benefits of data-driven decision-making in railway operations, improving reliability and safety by decreasing the need for reactive maintenance in hazardous environments. These initiatives have paved the way for further advanced analytics projects across Network Rail, fostering a more efficient, reliable, and passenger-focused railway system. This transformation highlights the power of integrated data strategies within the public sector.

Transition Indicators

If your company shows these signs, it is prepared to evolve to the last stage of modern data maturity. Here are some key indicators:

- **Consistent Use of Prescriptive Analytics**: If your company is automating decision-making processes across multiple departments using prescriptive analytics, it's a strong sign of maturity. This means you're not just predicting outcomes but also recommending actions based on data insights, enhancing efficiency and effectiveness.
- **Successful Data Monetization**: Implementing strategies that create new revenue from data assets shows a high level of data maturity. When you can generate income through data products or services, it shows that data is truly being leveraged as a strategic asset.
- **Deployment of Advanced Models**: Using AI and machine learning models in production environments with measurable business value demonstrates advanced capabilities. It's one thing to experiment with AI; it's another to integrate it into your operations and see tangible results.
- **Industry Recognition**: Being recognized as a leader in data-driven innovation and practices suggests that your company is setting industry standards. Awards, certifications, or media attention can validate your efforts and inspire continued investment in data initiatives.
- **Mature Governance Frameworks**: Successfully handling complex, multi-source data environments while maintaining high data quality is a key indicator. Robust governance ensures that, as you scale, your data remains reliable and compliant with regulations.

- **Agility in Data Strategy**: The ability to quickly adapt your data strategy to emerging technologies and market changes shows that your company is forward-thinking. This agility lets you stay ahead of competitors and respond effectively to new opportunities or threats.

Benefits and Limitations

Reaching the Strategic Stage offers significant benefits to your company. You gain a strong competitive advantage by leveraging data for strategic decision-making and innovation. With advanced analytics, you can quickly respond to market changes and customer needs, staying ahead of the curve. The data-driven culture fosters innovation across all levels, leading to improved operational efficiency and the discovery of new business opportunities.

However, there are limitations to consider. Managing the complexity of large-scale analytics initiatives can be challenging. As your data practices become more sophisticated, ethical and privacy concerns increase, requiring careful navigation to maintain trust and compliance. There's also a risk of over-reliance on data, potentially overlooking valuable human intuition and experience. Balancing data-driven insights with human judgment becomes crucial to avoid blind spots.

Key Focus Areas for Improvement

To address the challenges at this stage and continue advancing, focus on the following areas. These steps will help solidify your organization's position and prepare you for the next level of data maturity:

- **Integrate Prescriptive Analytics**: Enhance decision-making by automating complex tasks across business functions using prescriptive analytics. This increases efficiency and ensures consistent, data-driven actions throughout the business. For example, implementing prescriptive models in supply chain management can optimize inventory and reduce costs.

- **Scale Data Initiatives**: Expand your data projects into new business areas and explore emerging technologies for greater insights. By scaling initiatives, you can uncover opportunities that were previously untapped. Consider how integrating IoT data could revolutionize your product development or customer service strategies.
- **Strengthen Data Security**: Enhancing measures to protect data is critical as your data practices become more sophisticated. Invest in advanced security protocols and regular audits to safeguard against breaches. This protects your assets and maintains customer trust and regulatory compliance.
- **Invest in Advanced Technologies**: Maintain a competitive edge by adopting innovative tools like Generative AI and computer vision. These technologies can unlock new levels of analysis and operational capabilities. Staying current with technological advancements ensures you're not left behind as the industry evolves.
- **Develop Data Monetization Strategies**: Generate new revenue streams while upholding ethical guidelines by creating data products or services. This could involve offering analytics insights to clients or developing platforms that leverage your data assets. Monetizing data adds value and diversifies your income sources.
- **Foster Continuous Learning**: Promote ongoing training and encourage experimentation in data analytics. A culture of continuous learning keeps your team adaptable and innovative. Encourage employees to attend workshops, get certifications, or engage in cross-functional projects.
- **Enhance Cross-functional Collaboration**: Break down silos to ensure insights are effectively utilized across the company. Facilitating collaboration between departments can lead to more holistic solutions and drive data-driven innovation. Regular

interdepartmental meetings or shared platforms can foster this collaboration.

By focusing on these areas, your company can solidify its position at the Strategic Stage and prepare for the next level of data maturity. Remember, the data landscape always evolves, and staying ahead requires continuous effort and adaptation. The goal isn't just to use data effectively today but to build the capability to harness its power for whatever tomorrow brings.

Step 5: The Visionary Stage

Reaching the Visionary Stage is a monumental achievement. It's like standing at the peak of a mountain. You've mastered the climb and now have a panoramic view of what's possible. Your company doesn't just use data; it thrives on data-driven innovation. Have you ever imagined what it feels like to have data seamlessly integrated into every aspect of your business? Let's explore what this pinnacle of data maturity looks like.

Characteristics

Mindset

At this level, a data-driven culture is deeply embedded throughout the company. Data literacy isn't just for specialists; it's a core skill for everyone. Employees naturally turn to data when making decisions, and continuous learning keeps them ahead of the curve.

Leadership doesn't just support data initiatives; they champion them. Data strategy is integral to the organization's vision and mission. Leaders actively use data insights to drive strategic decisions and encourage experimentation with new data-driven approaches. It's an environment where innovation isn't just welcomed; it's expected.

People

Your organisation attracts and retains top data talent. Continuous professional development ensures skills stay relevant. Cross-functional teams leverage diverse expertise to solve complex data challenges.

Roles are well-defined, and data governance is integrated into all aspects of the organisation. There's a clear alignment between data practices and business objectives. Everyone knows their part in maintaining data integrity and contributing to success.

Process

Data governance is fully optimized, with agile processes that adapt to changing business needs. Proactive management ensures data policies and standards evolve together with the organisation. Imagine having a governance framework that is so flexible that it accommodates emerging technologies and data sources without missing a beat.

Data quality processes are automated and continuously refined. Real-time monitoring maintains impeccable data integrity. Advanced systems detect and address issues proactively. This means you can trust your data implicitly, which creates a foundation for making bold, informed decisions.

Tools and Technology

Your data infrastructure is highly advanced, leveraging the latest technologies for real-time processing, machine learning, and artificial intelligence. The architecture is flexible and scalable, quickly adapting to new data types and sources. Think of it as having a state-of-the-art toolkit that evolves with your needs.

You utilize cutting-edge analytics and business intelligence tools, enabling sophisticated analysis and real-time insights. Data-driven innovation isn't just a buzzword; it's a key differentiator in your market.

Advanced predictive and prescriptive analytics are integrated into decision-making processes at all levels.

Common Challenges

Even at the peak stage of data maturity, organizations face unique hurdles. Maintaining your position as a data leader requires continuous effort and adaptation. Let's explore some common challenges that Visionary Stage organizations often encounter:

- **Maintaining Agility and Innovation**: As operations scale, keeping processes agile while fostering innovation becomes increasingly complex. The structures that support large-scale operations can sometimes hinder quick adaptations and creative thinking. Balancing efficiency with flexibility is essential to stay ahead.
- **Aligning Data Governance with Rapid Advancements**: The fast pace of technological change means your data governance frameworks must continually evolve. Keeping policies up-to-date with emerging technologies and regulatory changes can be daunting. Falling behind could lead to compliance risks or slow adoption of beneficial innovations.
- **Competing for Top-Tier Talent**: Attracting and retaining the best data professionals is more competitive than ever. Other organizations vie for skilled talent, offering enticing packages and opportunities. Without a strong culture of innovation and growth, you might find it challenging to keep your top performers.
- **Balancing Innovation with Ethics**: Pushing the boundaries of data often raises ethical questions, especially around AI and machine learning. Ensuring that innovation doesn't come at the expense of privacy or ethical standards is crucial. Missteps can damage your reputation and erode public trust.

- **Ensuring Robust Security Measures**: High levels of data integration increase vulnerability to breaches. Implementing robust security protocols is essential as you handle more data across various platforms. A security breach can have far-reaching consequences, both legally and in terms of customer confidence.

Typical Data Initiatives

Organizations at the Visionary Stage engage in groundbreaking projects. Implementing AI-driven predictive maintenance across supply chains reduces downtime and optimizes resources. Real-time customer personalization using advanced machine learning has become the norm.

Establishing data marketplaces for secure data sharing and monetization opens new revenue streams. Implementing edge computing solutions for real-time processing in IoT environments allows for faster, more efficient decision-making right where data is generated.

Case Study: Ferrari's Digital Twin Initiative

In 2017, Scuderia Ferrari's partnership with Palantir Technologies was an excellent example of an innovative data initiative. Together, they implemented a digital twin solution that has revolutionized their Formula One racing operations. A digital twin is a virtual model that mirrors a physical system using real-time data.

This digital twin provided Ferrari with four key capabilities. First, it enabled integrated data analysis by consolidating information from thousands of sensors across aerodynamics, power units, and race engineering. Second, it facilitated rapid decision-making, allowing engineers to test new hypotheses on the fly. Pete May, Head of ERS

Design and Development, highlighted, 'There's a huge competitive advantage to being able to make decisions quickly.'

Third, the digital twin allowed for operational deployment, enabling swift implementation of decisions into racing operations. Finally, it created a continuous learning loop by capturing the outcomes of decisions and fostering ongoing improvements. These capabilities significantly reduced calculation times and enhanced Ferrari's ability to extract value from complex data sets. In 2024, Ferrari achieved first place in several races, showcasing how integrated data strategies can drive exceptional performance in Formula One racing.

Transition Indicators

Even though the Visionary Stage represents the highest level of data maturity, there are signs that indicate your company is solidifying its position and reaching the peak of this level:

- **Data-Driven Innovation as a Differentiator**: Your organisation leverages data to create new revenue streams or business models. This innovation sets you apart in the marketplace, making data a key component of your competitive advantage.
- **Recognition as an Industry Thought Leader**: You're not just keeping up with industry trends but setting them. Other organizations look to you for best practices in data and analytics. Your insights influence industry standards and shape the future of your field.
- **Pervasive Data Literacy**: Data literacy extends from entry-level employees to executives. Everyone understands and utilizes data in their day-to-day role, creating a unified language across the organisation. This widespread competence enhances collaboration and drives informed decision-making.
- **Agility in Adapting to Disruptions**: Your organisation can swiftly adjust its data strategy in response to market changes or

technological advancements. This agility demonstrates resilience and ensures you remain ahead of competitors who are slower to adapt.
- **Seamless Integration of Data Governance**: Data governance aligns effortlessly with business processes, maintaining compliance and quality without hindering innovation. This integration allows for continuous growth while ensuring data remains reliable and secure.

Benefits and Limitations

At this stage, you enjoy significant benefits. Data-driven innovation keeps you ahead of market trends and customer needs. Real-time insights and predictive analytics enable unparalleled agility. Operations are highly optimized, reducing costs through advanced analytics and AI across all functions.

However, maintaining this level of innovation requires constant investment in new technologies and skills. The rapidly evolving landscape means frequent updates to infrastructure and competencies. Balancing innovation with ethical considerations and privacy concerns becomes increasingly complex. High data integration can increase vulnerability to breaches, requiring robust security measures. There's also the pressure to continue finding new insights to justify the costs, which can lead to over-reliance on data at the expense of other decision-making forms.

Key Focus Areas for Improvement

To maintain your position at the forefront, and continue to push boundaries, focus on these critical areas:

- **Foster Continuous Innovation**: Encourage experimentation and calculated risk-taking. Create environments where teams can test new ideas and learn from failures. Remember, innovation thrives when learning is embraced.

- **Expand AI and Machine Learning Use**: Leverage advanced analytics for deeper insights and automate complex decisions. Moving beyond traditional approaches unlocks new potential.
- **Enhance Real-Time Processing**: Improve capabilities to support dynamic decision-making in rapidly changing environments. This allows you to react swiftly to market shifts and customer needs.
- **Strengthen Partnerships**: Collaborate to leverage external data and expertise. Participate in data-sharing initiatives, work with academic institutions, or form strategic alliances to tackle complex challenges collectively.

Like I said at the start at the beginning, reaching the Visionary Stage is remarkable, but the journey doesn't end here. As new technology emerges, new ways will unlock business value, so continuous improvement and adaptation are key to staying ahead. By focusing on these areas, you can maintain your competitive edge and continue to innovate in the ever-evolving data landscape.

Assessing Your Company's Data Landscape

Now that we've explored the five stages of data maturity, you might wonder, where does my organisation fit in this model? As mentioned in earlier chapters, understanding your organization's current situation is essential in building a solid data strategy.

To help you, I've created a detailed assessment tool. It checks how mature your company is in the four key components we've discussed before: mindset, people, process, and tools/technology, with each component having several sub-components, making a total of ten sub-components.

The assessment consists of carefully crafted questions that probe various aspects of your company's data practices. It's important to note that this assessment is a guideline, not a definitive measurement. It will, however, give you a solid understanding of your current data landscape. By reflecting on these questions, you'll gain insights into your strengths and areas needing improvement.

When assigning scores to each question, each question should be rated on a scale from 1 to 5:

1. **Not at All**: We have not implemented any measures in this area.
2. **Slightly**: We have begun to address this, but efforts could be more consistent.
3. **Moderately**: We have some established practices that must be consistently applied across the organisation.
4. **Considerably**: We have well-defined and consistent practices, but there's room for improvement.
5. **Fully**: We are fully optimized in this area, with well-established processes, widespread adoption, and ongoing improvements.

Alright, let's get started!

Mindset

Data Culture and Literacy

1) **Accessibility of Data:** How easily can employees access the data they need?
2) **Organizational Support:** To what extent does your company culture support and value data-driven practices?
3) **Decision-Making:** How often are decisions based on data insights rather than intuition?
4) **Training and Education:** How robust are your data training and education programs for all staff levels?

Data-Driven Leadership

5) **Executive Sponsorship:** Do senior leaders actively promote and support data initiatives?
6) **Strategic Alignment:** Are data initiatives aligned with your organization's business objectives and vision?

People

Talent and Skills

7) **Skill Availability:** Does your company have the necessary skills and expertise to manage and analyse data effectively?
8) **Role Clarity:** Are roles and responsibilities for data management clearly defined and assigned?
9) **Professional Development:** How committed is your company to ongoing training and development in data skills?

Collaboration and Communication

10) **Interdepartmental Collaboration:** How effective is communication between data teams and other departments?
11) **Data Stewardship:** Do you have designated data stewards or custodians responsible for data quality and governance?

Process

Data Governance

12) **Policy Definition:** How well-defined are your data governance policies and standards?
13) **Lifecycle Management:** Does your company effectively manage data from creation to disposal?
14) **Regulatory Compliance:** How compliant are you with data privacy regulations, and how proactively do you manage data-related risks?

Data Quality

15) **Accuracy:** How accurate is the data used for decision-making?
16) **Completeness:** Is your data comprehensive and free from significant gaps?
17) **Consistency:** How consistent is data across different systems and departments?

Tools & Technology

Data Architecture and Infrastructure

18) **Data Collection Efficiency:** How efficient and automated are your data collection processes?
19) **Systems Integration:** How well are your data systems integrated to allow seamless data flow?
20) **Storage Solutions:** How reliable and scalable are your data storage solutions?
21) **Modern Technologies:** To what extent are you utilizing modern data technologies like cloud platforms, big data tools, or AI?

Analytics and Business Intelligence

22) **Tool Accessibility:** How accessible are advanced analytics and BI tools to those who need them?
23) **Advanced Analytics Usage:** Are you utilizing predictive or prescriptive analytics to inform strategy?
24) **Data Visualization:** How effective are your data visualization capabilities in conveying insights clearly and compellingly?

Data Security & Privacy

25) **Security Measures:** How robust are your data security protocols against breaches and unauthorized access?
26) **Privacy Compliance:** How compliant is your company with data privacy laws like GDPR or CCPA?
27) **Risk Management:** How well do you identify and manage data-related risks?
28) **Encryption and Protection:** How comprehensive are your data encryption and protection processes?

Data Management Tools

29) **Storage Solutions:** How reliable and efficient are your data storage solutions?
30) **Processing Systems:** How efficient are your data processing systems?
31) **Tool Integration:** How well do your data management tools integrate with other enterprise systems?

Putting It All Together

After completing the assessment, it's time to interpret your results. Follow these steps to calculate your scores:

1. **Sub-Component Score:** Tally your scores for each sub-component and calculate the average.

2. **Component Score:** Take the average of each sub-component score to get the score for each of the four key components.
3. **Overall Maturity Score:** Take the average for each component score to get your organization's overall maturity score.

To interpret where each of your sub-component scores, component scores, and overall organizational scores sit within the maturity model, refer to the following mapping of scores to their respective stages:

1. **Emerging Stage (1 to 1.5):** Your data practices are just beginning to develop.
2. **Empowered Stage (1.5 to 2.5):** You have some foundational data initiatives in place.
3. **Integrated Stage (2.5 to 3.5):** Your data efforts are more cohesive and strategically aligned.
4. **Strategic Stage (3.5 to 4.5):** Data plays a key role in your strategic decision-making.
5. **Visionary Stage (4.5 to 5):** Your company leads with data-driven innovation and continuous improvement.

Using the Assessment to Push Forward Your Data Strategy

We'll use the assessment results as the foundation for the next four steps of the data strategy framework. The data strategy will ensure we develop a structured and coordinated approach to improving data maturity. In the meantime, you should use the assessment results to:

1. **Identify Gaps**: The scores highlight areas where your company may lag. For example, a low score in data governance signals a need to establish or refine your policies. Assemble cross-functional teams to ensure solutions are implemented effectively and align with the overall business goals.
2. **Prioritize Initiatives**: Not all gaps are equal. Focus on areas that align with your business objectives and offer the greatest

return on investment. Basically, the quick wins. If improving data quality will directly enhance customer satisfaction, it should be a top priority.
3. **Benchmarking**: Compare your scores against industry benchmarks or past assessments to measure progress. This helps you understand where you stand relative to competitors and track improvements over time.

Assessing your data maturity is more than just a diagnostic exercise; it's critical to guide your organization's evolution. Remember, this assessment is a guideline, not a definitive measurement. It provides a solid understanding of your current data landscape, helping you make informed decisions on how to proceed with the next steps in the data strategy framework; determining where to invest time, resources, and effort. Use the assessment periodically to ensure the strategy adapts to changing business needs and technological advancements.

Your Data Maturity Self-Assessment

For a PDF copy of the Data Maturity Self-Assessment, please follow this link: https://wissenlau.com/data-maturity-assessment or scan the QR code below:

Summary

In this chapter, we dived into the heart of understanding your organization's data maturity. We explored every stage in the data maturity in detail, from the initial Emerging Stage to the Visionary Stage. In each stage, we discussed the four key components (mindset, people, processes, and technology), common challenges, type of data initiatives, what transition looks like, benefits and limitations, and how to improve and move to the next stage.

To help you assess where your company stand, I introduced a detailed self-assessment tool tailored to leaders like you. The questionnaire sheds light on your organization's strengths and weaknesses. You can gain valuable insights into your current data landscape by reflecting on the four key components and ten sub-components. This will help you build the foundation for the next four steps in the data strategy framework. In the meantime, where does your company stand in the data maturity model?

Thank you so much for making it this far!

I really appreciate the time you took to read my book. As a small, individual publisher, it means a lot and I hope to make a positive impact for you and your company.

If you have 60 seconds, it'll mean the world to me if you share your honest feedback on Amazon. It does wonders for the book, and I love hearing your thoughts and experience with it!

To leave your feedback:

1) Open your camera app.
2) Point your mobile device at the QR code below.
3) This will open a review page in your browser app.

OR

Visit Link: wissenlau.com/sdp-feedback

THANK YOU!

Part 2:
Building the Necessary Capabilities

Chapter 4:
Cultivating a Data-Driven Mindset

In this chapter, we'll cover the principles and actionable steps around mindset, the first component in step 3 of the data strategy - growing a data-driven culture.

As mentioned in earlier chapters, data is a critical asset for driving growth, innovation, and competitive advantage. However, simply having vast amounts of data is not enough. The true power of data is unlocked when an organisation cultivates a data-driven mindset. This collective attitude prioritises data in every decision-making process and seamlessly aligns data initiatives with overarching business objectives.

A data-driven mindset shapes how organisations perceive and utilise their data assets. It transforms data initiatives from isolated technical projects into integrated components of the business strategy, ensuring that accurate, relevant, and timely data insights inform every decision.

Defining a Data-Driven Mindset

At its core, a data-driven mindset embodies these key attributes:

1. **Strategic Thinking About Data**: Evaluating data through the lens of the organisation's broader goals. Decisions are not made just for short-term gains but with a long-term vision that aligns with the company's mission and objectives.
2. **Critical Analysis**: Encouraging individuals to question the accuracy and relevance of data. This means not accepting information at face value but delving deeper to understand its origins, context, and implications.
3. **Continuous Focus on Data**: Making data a central component at every stage of decision-making. It shouldn't just be used selectively or sporadically, but instead, it should be used as a consistent element for strategizing, planning, and executing initiatives.
4. **Understanding Data Limitations**: Recognising that while data is powerful, it doesn't hold all the answers. A balanced approach considers other qualitative factors and acknowledges nuances that data alone may not capture.

The Role and Importance of Mindset

Cultivating a data-driven mindset is pivotal for several reasons. Firstly, when data informs decisions at all organisational levels, outcomes are more likely to be objective, strategic, and aligned with business goals. Secondly, a unified mindset ensures that data efforts directly support and enhance the company's strategy, maximising the return on data investments. Thirdly, embedding a data-driven mindset fosters a culture of continuous learning and improvement, encouraging collaboration, innovation, and a proactive approach to challenges.

Despite the clear benefits, many organisations need help fully embracing a data-driven mindset. A study by McKinsey revealed that only 30% of organisations align their data strategy with their overall business strategy, indicating a significant opportunity for improvement. This gap underscores the need for leaders to actively promote and cultivate this mindset to realise the full potential of their data assets.

Common Challenges

Moving to a data-driven mindset isn't straightforward. Many organisations face hurdles that can slow down or even halt progress. Recognising these challenges is the first step in achieving successful adoption.

Resistance to Change

Change often makes people uneasy, especially in companies with long-standing practices. You might find employees clinging to familiar methods, worried that new data-driven approaches will disrupt their routines or devalue their expertise. It's comfortable to stick with what we know, isn't it?

Fear of the unknown plays a big role here. Introducing data-driven processes can stir anxiety about job security or the need to learn new skills. Long-time staff may wonder if they can adapt to new technologies or methodologies. They might even fear that increased data transparency could expose flaws in their performance.

So, how do we overcome this resistance? Clear communication is key. You must highlight the benefits of embracing data-driven practices and reassure your team they'll have the support they need during the transition. Involving them in the process can also foster a sense of ownership and acceptance.

Lack of Data Literacy

Another significant barrier is the general lack of data literacy within the organisation. If your employees don't understand basic data concepts, they may feel intimidated by new initiatives. Have you ever sat through a meeting where jargon like 'confusion matrix' or 'mean absolute error' flew over your head? It's alienating, right?

This skills gap isn't limited to entry-level staff; some executives also struggle to leverage data effectively. Without proper understanding, there's a risk of misinterpreting data, leading to misguided decisions that could harm the business.

To tackle this, investing in training is essential. Simplify complex concepts and encourage a culture where asking questions is welcomed. Providing accessible resources and practical examples can demystify data and empower your team to engage with confidence.

Limited Leadership Advocacy

The leadership team sets the tone for any cultural shift. If leaders don't demonstrate data-driven behaviours, expecting employees to follow suit is hard. Imagine if decisions are made based on gut feelings rather than data; what kind of message does that send to your team?

When there are inconsistencies between what leaders say and do, it can create scepticism. Employees may doubt the organisation's commitment if leadership vocalises support for data initiatives but doesn't participate actively. Additionally, without strong advocacy, data projects might lack the necessary resources or attention, limiting their impact.

As such, leaders need to walk the talk. By visibly supporting data initiatives and integrating data into their own decision-making processes, they can inspire the rest of the organisation. Leadership training on data literacy can also enhance their ability to lead by example.

Trust and Transparency Issues

For all data initiatives, employees need to build trust before embracing them. Doubts about the data's accuracy are a common challenge. If there has been inconsistent or inaccurate data in the past, scepticism is only natural. Would you rely on data you don't trust?

A lack of transparent data practices can further erode trust. It creates suspicion if employees aren't clear on how data is collected, analysed, or used. Concerns about privacy, ethics, or potential misuse may also surface, especially with those 'black-box' machine learning models that are hard to understand.

To build trust, you need rigorous validation processes and transparent data practices. Communicate openly about how data is handled and involve your team in developing data policies. Clear explanations can go a long way in building confidence and acceptance.

The first step toward cultivating a data-driven mindset is recognising these common challenges. Overcoming them requires a focused effort on key principles that drive mindset-related change. In the next section, we'll explore various principles that'll play a pivotal role in building a more data-driven mindset within your organisation.

Principle 1: Leadership and Advocacy

Fostering a data-driven mindset starts at the very top. As leaders, you set the tone for your entire organisation. Your commitment to data doesn't just influence policies; it shapes the culture. By actively championing data initiatives and integrating data-driven goals into your company's vision, you transform how your team perceives and utilises data.

Leadership Commitment

Have you ever noticed how your team's attitude mirrors your own? When you prioritise data, your team is more likely to follow suit. You align data initiatives with your organisation's mission by articulating a clear and compelling vision for a data-driven future. Imagine using data science to predict customer needs. This won't just boost customer satisfaction, but also demonstrate the strategic value of data in achieving your goals.

Investing in data initiatives shows your commitment. Allocate budgets for data infrastructure and tools. Providing time and resources for data literacy training. Dedicate people to data-focused roles. Separate data from IT and appoint roles such as Chief Data Officer. You want to send a strong message that data matters here, that it isn't just an IT concern but a strategic asset requiring dedicated leadership.

But commitment goes beyond just allocating resources. It would help if you led by example too. When you use data to inform your own decisions, you set a precedent. Share insights from data that influenced major strategies. Highlight successful outcomes resulting from data-driven approaches. When your team sees you making decisions based on data, it reinforces the expectation that they should do the same.

Actionable Steps for Driving Data Culture

Allocate Resources Strategically

Resources are not just budgets. They also include time, tools and talent.

1. **Invest in Infrastructure:** Allocate funds for necessary data tools and technologies. Whether it's advanced analytics software or cloud storage solutions, ensure your team has what they need.

2. **Dedicate Colleagues:** Assign skilled individuals to data roles. This might mean hiring data scientists or upskilling current employees.
3. **Provide Training Time:** Allow team members time for data literacy training during work hours. This shows you value their development and the importance of data skills.

Communicate the Vision Consistently

As the saying goes, out of sight, out of mind. Keep a data-driven mindset in your organisation's mind.

1. **Regular Updates:** Provide frequent updates on data initiatives and progress towards goals.
2. **Host Conferences:** Host data-related conferences where employees can discuss data initiatives across the business and wider industry.
3. **Visual Reminders:** Use infographics or dashboards to display key data metrics and achievements in communal areas.

Align Incentives with Data Goals

Colleagues are more responsive to incentives that align with organisational priorities.

1. **Incorporate Data Metrics in Evaluations:** Include data utilisation as a criterion in performance reviews.
2. **Reward Data-Driven Behaviours:** Offer bonuses or recognition for teams that effectively use data to drive results.
3. **Set Department Data Objectives:** Encourage each department to set its own data goals that align with the company's overall strategy.

Case Study: Amazon's Obsession With Their Customers

Jeff Bezos introduced Amazon's 'empty chair' strategy to prioritise customer data in decision-making. The empty chair symbolised the customer during meetings, reminding leaders to consider their insights. This visual cue encouraged the analysis of customer behaviour data and fostered a data-driven, customer-centric culture. As a result, Amazon improved customer experiences and drove growth by ensuring that data about customer needs and preferences guided strategies and operations. This simple yet effective metaphor helped instil a data-driven mindset across the organisation, contributing significantly to Amazon's success in the e-commerce market.

Change Management

Shifting to a data-driven mindset isn't just about policies, but the people. Change can be unsettling. Have you ever felt uneasy when a new system or process was introduced? Your team will most likely feel the same. Involving employees at all levels eases this transition. You foster a sense of ownership and collaboration by forming cross-functional teams to identify data needs and opportunities.

Clear communication is essential. You want to explain why the change is happening and how it benefits the company and your employees. Tailor your message to different departments. For example, show marketing how data analytics can help improve brand awareness. Show operations how data can streamline processes and increase productivity.

Provide ample training and support. Offer data literacy programs and accessible resources. Encourage a culture where asking questions is welcomed. When your team feels supported, they're more likely to embrace new practices confidently.

Actionable Steps for Leading Change

Develop a Comprehensive Roadmap

Change doesn't happen overnight. You'll need a thought-through plan to guide you and your organisation through the transition.

1. **Set Milestones:** Break down the journey into manageable chunks. For example, start with data literacy training, then implement data visualisation tools.
2. **Assign Responsibilities:** Clearly define who is accountable for each task. This could be department heads or project managers.
3. **Anticipate Challenges:** Identify potential obstacles, such as resistance from certain teams, and plan how to address them.
4. **Establish Success Metrics:** Decide how you'll measure progress. This might include the number of employees trained or an increase in data-driven decisions.

Communicate Transparently and Frequently

Keep everyone informed to reduce uncertainty.

1. **Explain the 'Why':** Share the reasons behind the shift to a data-driven culture.
2. **Share Success Stories:** Highlight early wins to build momentum and show tangible benefits.
3. **Maintain Open Dialogue:** Encourage questions and be honest about challenges and how you address them.

Invest Heavily in Training and Development

Provide your team with all the skills they need to excel.

1. **Offer Tailored Training Programs:** Create training materials with data that teams already know. For sales teams, use customer data. For HR, people and talent management data should be used.

2. **Provide Ongoing Support:** Establish mentorship programs where more data-savvy employees can guide others.
3. **Utilise Various Learning Platforms:** Cater to different learning styles by combining online courses, physical workshops, and interactive sessions.

Advocacy

As leaders of your organisation, your advocacy doesn't stop at just initiating change; it continues by actively promoting and sustaining it. Communicate the strategic value of data initiatives regularly. Share success stories that highlight the impact of data-driven decisions. This keeps momentum going and reinforces the importance of data in everyday operations.

Recognise and reward those who embrace data-driven practices. Implement recognition programs. Highlight achievements in company communications. Consider data utilisation in performance evaluations. This motivates individuals and signals to the entire organisation that data matters.

Embedding data into your company's values and norms solidifies its importance. Update your organisational values to include data-driven decision-making explicitly. Model these behaviours yourself. Integrate data literacy into onboarding and ongoing training. Establish 'data champions' in different departments to promote best practices and serve as local advocates.

Actionable Steps for Advocating Data Culture

Recognise and Reward Data-Driven Achievements

Positive reinforcement goes a long way.

1. **Implement Recognition Programs:** Create awards for teams or individuals who use data effectively. It's also a good reason to share positivity and PR across the company.
2. **Public Acknowledgement:** Celebrate achievements in company-wide communication or meetings.
3. **Link Rewards to Business Goals:** Ensure recognition highlights how data-driven efforts contribute to the overall business strategy.

Ensure Continuous Learning and Improvement

Fostering a data-driven culture is a marathon, not a sprint.

1. **Offer Advanced Training:** As your team develops their skills, provide opportunities to learn more sophisticated data techniques.
2. **Stay Updated on Trends:** Stay up to date with emerging data technologies and consider how they might benefit your organisation.
3. **Seek Ongoing Feedback:** Regularly ask your team how to improve data initiatives and act on their suggestions.

By building on these actionable steps, you'll develop a practical roadmap to foster a data-driven mindset within your organisation. Remember, transforming culture takes time and consistent effort. However, it's heavily dependent on you. With strong leadership and a clear vision, you can lead your company into a future where data isn't just another tool but a strategic asset and a cornerstone of your company's success.

Principle 2: Cultivating Data Literacy

Building a data-driven culture isn't just about having the latest technology or data assets. It's about making sure everyone in your organisation understands the importance of data, especially when it comes to insight and innovation. This creates a collective mindset that drives continuous improvement and competitive advantages.

Encouraging Curiosity and Critical Thinking

One of the key components in strengthening a data-driven mindset is encouraging curiosity and critical thinking. When you motivate your team to explore and question, they turn data into actionable insights. Have you ever noticed how the best ideas often come from someone asking the right questions? Encouraging your team to dive deeper into data will unlock potential innovations that'll drive your business forward. In a recent role, I identified potential saving opportunities in the first few weeks of joining. After building a simulation with my team, we estimated it would save the supply chain operation around £2m+ per year.

Actionable Steps for Encouraging Curiosity and Critical Thinking

Promote a Culture of Inquiry

Building an environment where questions are welcomed encourages deeper understanding and innovation.

1. **Recognise Inquisitive Thinking**: Acknowledge and reward employees who ask insightful questions or challenge existing processes.
2. **Organise Data Challenges**: Host events where teams solve real business problems using data, stimulating creative thinking.
3. **Encourage Open Discussions**: Create forums or meetings where employees can share ideas and explore data-driven solutions.

Create a Data Innovation Submission Process

Providing a formal channel for ideas empowers employees to contribute to data initiatives.

1. **Establish an Internal Portal**: Set up a platform where team members can submit data-driven ideas or improvements.
2. **Facilitate Cross-Department Collaboration**: Encourage feedback and collaboration across different teams on submitted ideas.
3. **Streamline Idea Evaluation**: Implement a clear process for reviewing and acting on proposals to maintain momentum.

Host Regular 'Data Exploration' Workshops

Hands-on experiences deepen understanding and spark innovation.

1. **Provide Guidance from Data Experts**: Have data professionals lead workshops to mentor and inspire employees.
2. **Focus on Real Data**: Use actual company data to make the experience relevant and impactful.
3. **Encourage Hypothesis Testing**: Allow employees to test their ideas and see firsthand how data can inform decisions.

Support Experimentation with Data

Allowing time and resources for experimentation encourages innovation.

1. **Allocate Time for Innovation**: Set aside dedicated hours for employees to explore data beyond their daily tasks.
2. **Host Hackathons or Pilot Projects**: Organise events where teams can creatively tackle challenges using data.
3. **Provide Resources for Testing Ideas**: Offer access to datasets and tools needed for experimentation.

Case Study: DBS's 'Data Heros' Initiative

DBS Bank initiated a data upskilling program called 'Data Heroes' over 18 months, training more than 16,000 employees in big data and data analytics. The goal? Empower their team to tackle business challenges, spot new opportunities, and work seamlessly with data scientists and technology teams. The program offered a comprehensive curriculum tailored to different skill levels, allowing everyone to learn at their own pace. This flexibility ensured all employees, from beginners to advanced users, could benefit. As a result, teams were able to automate reports and deliver more actionable insights, boosting overall performance.

Empowering Employees with Support and Resources

To truly embed a data-driven mindset, you must empower your employees with the right tools and support. Have you ever tried to complete a task without the proper resources? It's frustrating, isn't it? When your team has access to user-friendly data tools and comprehensive training, they become more engaged and effective in their roles. This empowerment fosters innovation, boosts morale, and accelerates the adoption of data-centric practices across your organisation.

Actionable Steps for Empowering Employees

Provide Access to User-Friendly Data Tools

Equipping your team with the right tools makes data exploration accessible and efficient.

1. **Ensure Widespread Accessibility**: Make sure these tools are available to all relevant team members, not just a select few.
2. **Offer Tool Training Sessions**: Provide training to help employees become comfortable with new software.

Offer Comprehensive Training Programs

Tailored training empowers employees to use data confidently in their roles.

1. **Develop Role-Specific Training**: Customise programs to address the unique needs of different departments.
2. **Utilise Various Learning Formats**: Offer online courses and workshops to cater to different learning styles: visual, auditory, read/write, and touch.
3. **Provide Ongoing Support**: Establish resources like help desks or mentorship programs for continuous learning.

Encourage Collaboration Across Teams

Collaboration fosters knowledge sharing and sparks innovation.

1. **Build Cross-Functional Teams**: Bring employees from various departments together to work on data projects.
2. **Promote Knowledge Sharing**: Encourage teams to share their insights and successes with the wider organisation.
3. **Facilitate Communication Channels**: Use collaborative tools to make it easy for teams to share data and collaborate.

Promoting Data-Driven Decision Making

Once your team becomes more comfortable with data, introducing data into your decision-making process is the next step. Integrate data analysis into standard workflows. For instance, when making proposals, ask for data-backed justifications. This helps make data a natural part of daily operations.

Establish decision frameworks that require data validation. Define the data needed for different decisions and set clear processes for gathering and analysing it. This standardises how decisions are made and ensures consistency across the board.

Accountability is crucial too. You should track and review decisions to see if data insights support them and evaluate the outcomes. This promotes transparency and helps your team learn and improve over time. How many projects, especially in the past, have you made decisions based on a hunch that didn't pan out? Using data will help prevent those costly missteps.

Actionable Steps for Data-Driven Decisions

Integrate Data into Daily Processes

Making data a natural part of everyday work reinforces its importance in decision-making.

1. **Standardise Data Use in Meetings**: All reports and presentations must include relevant data to support key points.
2. **Implement Data Review Stages**: Before finalising decisions, incorporate a step where data is analysed and discussed.
3. **Utilise Dashboards**: Give teams real-time access to important metrics through user-friendly dashboards.

Develop Clear Decision-Making Frameworks

Establishing guidelines ensures everyone follows the same process when making decisions.

1. **Outline Data Requirements**: Specify what data type is needed for various decisions. This might include customer feedback, sales figures, or market trends.
2. **Create Simple Guidelines**: Develop easy-to-follow processes for collecting and analysing data. Keep it straightforward to encourage use.
3. **Train Teams on Frameworks**: Offer workshops to ensure everyone understands how to apply these frameworks effectively.

Enhance Accountability and Transparency

Holding teams accountable promotes trust and encourages responsible use of data.

1. **Monitor Outcomes**: Track the results of decisions to see how data influences the outcomes. This can provide valuable lessons for the future.
2. **Hold Post-Decision Reviews**: Discuss what went well and what could be improved in the decision-making process.
3. **Encourage Open Dialogue**: Promote a culture where team members feel comfortable sharing their experiences, including challenges.

Enhancing data literacy, encouraging continuous learning, and embedding data into your decision-making processes will cultivate a robust data-driven mindset within your organisation. This empowers your team to make more informed decisions, drive innovation, and fuel business growth.

Ultimately, nurturing a data-driven mindset unlocks the full potential of your data assets and gives your organisation a competitive advantage in an increasingly data-centric world.

Case Study: Foxton's Embedded Data-Driven Culture

Foxtons, a leading UK estate agency, built a sustainable data-driven culture with a comprehensive strategy. They use interactive dashboards displayed prominently in offices, showing real-time KPIs and team-specific metrics. This visibility helps you track performance across the customer journey, from lead generation to deal conversions. By making data accessible, Foxtons fosters informed decision-making, quick trend identification, and healthy competition. CEO Guy Gittins emphasised that this approach prepares them for future challenges. Additionally, Foxtons boosted training tenfold, enhancing data literacy and empowering employees to use data effectively. This integration drives continuous improvement and performance.

Principle 3: Trust and Transparency

Building a data-driven culture is more than just collecting data or having the hard skills to interpret it. It's about fostering trust and transparency around that data. How can your team make informed decisions if they don't trust the information they're given? Have you ever hesitated to adopt a new system because you weren't sure how it would impact your existing teams? Understanding and addressing common barriers to change is crucial for creating an environment where data-driven practices can thrive.

Identifying Common Barriers to Change

Resistance to change is a natural human response, especially when it involves shifting familiar routines or learning new skills. To successfully embed a data-driven mindset, it's essential to identify and understand the barriers that may hold your organisation back. These obstacles can range from individual apprehensions to systemic issues within the company. By recognising these challenges, you can develop targeted strategies to address them, ensuring a smoother transition to a data-centric culture.

On an individual level, you might encounter employees who don't like change, feel threatened by new data processes, or don't see how data fits into their daily roles. They might worry about being replaced or fear increased data transparency could expose shortcomings. On an organisational level, common barriers include silos between departments, data privacy concerns, and a general lack of data literacy. Ignoring these barriers can slow down or even derail your data initiatives.

Actionable Steps for Identifying and Overcoming Barriers

Assess Employee Sentiments

Understanding how your employees feel about data initiatives is the first step in addressing resistance.

1. **Conduct Surveys or Interviews**: Use anonymous surveys or one-on-one interviews to gather honest feedback about their perceptions and concerns regarding data changes.
2. **Analyse Feedback for Common Themes**: Find response patterns indicating widespread issues or misunderstandings.
3. **Address Misconceptions Promptly**: Use the insights gained to clarify misunderstandings and provide reassurance where needed.

Examine Organisational Structures

Identifying structural barriers helps plan effective strategies to promote data sharing and collaboration.

1. **Map Out Data Silos**: Identify where data is isolated within departments and how this limits organisational effectiveness.
2. **Review Current Practices**: Analyse existing workflows that might hinder data sharing or create resistance to change.
3. **Develop Cross-Department Initiatives**: Create projects that encourage collaboration and break down silos.

Learn From Past Change Initiatives

Leveraging lessons from previous changes can prevent repeating the same mistakes.

1. **Review Previous Organisational Changes**: Analyse past initiatives to identify what worked and what didn't.

2. **Identify Sources of Resistance**: Understand why resistance occurred previously, was it due to lack of communication, insufficient training, or other factors?
3. **Apply Lessons Learned**: Incorporate these insights into your current data initiatives to mitigate similar issues.

Provide Support and Resources

Offering the necessary support can alleviate fears and facilitate the adoption of new practices.

1. **Offer Comprehensive Training Programs**: Provide tailored training to improve data literacy across all levels.
2. **Establish Help Desks or Support Teams**: Set up resources where employees can get assistance with new tools or processes.
3. **Set Realistic Expectations**: Be transparent about the timeline and effort required for the transition.

Case Study: AstraZeneca's Cross-Functional Real-World Evidence Initiative

AstraZeneca, a leading pharmaceutical company, needed clarification regarding data governance and integrating real-world evidence (RWE) into their decision-making processes. Many teams perceived RWE as overly complex and irrelevant, resulting in resistance to a unified data strategy. To overcome this, AstraZeneca established a dedicated group focused on RWE, uniting biostatisticians, epidemiologists, health economists, and programmers from various departments.

This collaborative approach fostered open dialogue and knowledge sharing, enhancing data integration and analytical capabilities. The initiative enabled AstraZeneca to evaluate product cost-effectiveness better and gain deeper insights into healthcare outcomes that traditional methods had previously missed. Ultimately, this cross-departmental effort transformed initial scepticism into a robust data-driven culture, leading to more informed strategies and improved patient outcomes.

Promoting Transparency in Data Processes

Trust isn't just limited to quality; it's also about knowing how data is collected and used. Have you ever wondered where a piece of data came from or how it was processed? Lack of transparency can breed suspicion and hinder the adoption of data-driven practices.

Being open about your data processes helps build trust. Share how data is collected, the methods used for analysis, and how decisions are made based on that data. When your team understands the journey from raw data to actionable insight, they're more likely to trust the results.

Maintain accessible documentation. Provide data dictionaries and records that explain data sources and lineage; basically, what steps were taken to get the data from the source to the current destination. This transparency allows anyone to trace back and understand the origins of the data they use.

Develop clear data policies on usage, privacy, and governance. Outline acceptable uses of data and how personal information is protected. Communicate these policies to ensure everyone knows their responsibilities.

Actionable Steps for Enhancing Transparency

Publish Data Catalogues

Making data assets visible helps stakeholders understand and utilise available resources.

1. **Create an Inventory of Data Assets**: List all available datasets with descriptions and purposes.

2. **Include Access Information**: Provide details on how to find and use each dataset.
   3. **Update the Catalogue Regularly**: Keep information current to maintain its usefulness.

Encourage a Culture of Data Sharing

Promoting data sharing fosters collaboration and innovation.

   1. **Promote Collaborative Tools**: Use platforms that facilitate easy data sharing among teams.
   2. **Recognise Sharing Efforts**: Acknowledge teams that actively share valuable data.
   3. **Break Down Silos**: Encourage cross-departmental projects to foster collaboration.

Fostering Open Communication About Data

Open communication is the lifeblood of a data-driven culture. Without it, misconceptions can arise, and trust can wane. Have you ever felt out of the loop on a project? It's not a good feeling.

Establish channels for feedback. Allow your team to express concerns or suggestions about data practices. This could be through suggestion boxes, dedicated email addresses, or regular meetings.

Provide regular updates on data initiatives. Keep everyone informed about changes, successes, and challenges. This transparency helps maintain engagement and shows that data is a priority.

Encourage dialogue across all levels of the organisation. Host workshops, Q&A sessions, or peer learning events. When everyone feels included, collaboration flourishes.

Actionable Steps for Strengthening Communication

Foster a Culture of Openness

An open culture encourages trust and transparency at all levels.

1. **Lead by Example**: Encourage leaders to be transparent about data initiatives and decisions.
2. **Promote Open Dialogue**: Create an environment where questions and discussions about data are welcomed.
3. **Address Concerns Promptly**: Tackle issues or misunderstandings quickly to maintain trust.

By focusing on trust and transparency, you're addressing the root causes of resistance to data adoption. It's essential to ensure data quality, promote transparent processes, and foster open communication. When your team trusts the data and understands how it's used, they're more likely to embrace it. This paves the way for innovation, efficiency, and sustained business growth. Ultimately, you're not just implementing a data strategy but building a competitive advantage in the marketplace.

Case Study: General Electric's 'Voice of the Customer' Program

General Electric launched the 'Voice of the Customer' program to cultivate a data-driven culture and enhance customer retention. They facilitated open communication using surveys and interviews to gather real-time feedback on their industrial solutions. GE encouraged knowledge sharing by distributing this feedback across departments, allowing teams to integrate customer insights into their decisions. Although not explicitly stated, the program recognises and acts on contributions from customers and employees. As a result, GE saw a 20% increase in customer retention over five years. This initiative demonstrates how integrating feedback can drive growth and foster a data-driven mindset within an organisation.

Summary

Developing a data-driven mindset is a transformative journey that redefines your organisation's culture and operations. The collective mindset significantly impacts the success of data initiatives, and strong leadership drives this change by setting a precedent that data is a critical asset to be integrated into every decision. Leaders inspire adoption across all levels by advocating for a data-driven approach. Enhancing data literacy empowers your entire team, making data accessible and actionable for everyone, not just analysts. Continuous learning and transparent practices build the foundations of a sustainable data-driven culture, ensuring that data is utilised and relied upon confidently, fostering an environment where open communication and collaboration thrive.

As you embrace this shift, proactively cultivate a data-driven mindset, starting at the leadership level. Invest in your people by allocating resources to develop data literacy and empower employees. Commit to openness by building trust through transparent communication and data practices. These steps strengthen your organisation's internal capabilities and position it ahead in an increasingly data-centric world.

By applying these actionable steps, you'll unlock the full potential of your data assets and propel your organisation forward. Remember, the journey to becoming truly data-driven is ongoing, but with commitment and the right mindset, the rewards are substantial. Next, we'll move on to the 'people' component of building a data-driven culture.

Chapter 5:
Empowering Your People

This chapter will discuss the 'people' part, the second component of implementing a robust data strategy. Like building a data-driven culture, ensuring your team has the right skills and experience ensures you have the right people to ensure your ideas happen.

While tools and processes are important, it's the people who really make a data strategy work. They look at data, find useful information, and make smart choices that help the business grow. Without skilled and motivated people, even the best data plans can miss their goals.

Defining the People Component

At its heart, the people component focuses on:

1. **Talent Acquisition:** It's important to bring in people with the right data skills and the right way of thinking. This means looking for experts like data scientists or cloud architects who do their jobs well and fit the company's goals and culture. Hiring the right people is just the first step.
2. **Workforce Development:** Once you find the right individuals, you must keep teaching them new things. Offering ongoing training helps your team stay updated with the latest data tools and methods. This way, your team can improve and adapt to new changes in the data world.
3. **Skill Application:** Your team can use their knowledge to look at data and find important insights. They can understand complex information, spot trends, and help make decisions that match your business objectives.
4. **Change Agents:** Motivated employees help spread good data practices throughout the company. By encouraging others to use data, they help everyone become better at understanding and using data in their daily work.

People are the heart of a successful data strategy. When employees are skilled, motivated, and engaged, they turn data into useful insights that help the business grow. They ensure that data projects are not just technical tasks but important parts of the company's overall plan. This teamwork and dedication ensures that every decision is backed by the right information at the right time.

The Role and Importance of Empowering People

Investing in your team is critical in successfully implementing a robust data strategy. When employees have the right skills and feel motivated, they can turn ideas into meaningful results for your business. They use their knowledge to solve tricky data problems and develop new ways to help your business grow. Hiring people who know about data and share the company's goals ensures your team can do great work with data initiatives.

A smart and skilled team will help your company stay ahead. These employees don't just follow the rules; they set new standards. These teams understand both the business and technical sides, which helps them find new chances to improve. For example, I worked with a client that sends out engineers to inspect assets and write reports on a regular basis. I worked on an initiative that used machine learning techniques to extract meaning from these reports and created heat maps and trends that helped the client plan better, saving them lots of money. I recommend changes in reporting to maximize the benefits of the solution. Keeping your team trained with the latest data tools and methods will ensure your company stays current and can handle new data challenges.

When employees feel empowered, they help the whole company get better at using data. Their enthusiasm encourages everyone to use data in their work, creating a company-wide love for data. This builds a culture where smart decisions are made using data, aligning with the company's big goals and helping projects run smoothly. Motivated employees are more likely to support and spread a data-focused way of working, ensuring data is always a key part of the company's plans and actions.

Even though a great team is so important, many companies forget to focus on their people and spend more on technology instead. You make sure your data plan works well by hiring the right people, helping them grow, and keeping them happy. Balancing new technology with ongoing training and a strong data culture helps your company use data in the best way possible, leading to new ideas and staying ahead of competitors.

Common Challenges

Building a strong data team isn't easy. Many companies face problems that can stall or even detail their efforts to empower their people effectively. Knowing these problems is the first step to fixing them.

Skill Gaps and Shortages

Finding the right people for data jobs is like searching for a needle in a haystack. There aren't enough skilled data workers, which makes it tough for companies to hire data analysts, data scientists, or engineers. Even basic data skills are missing in many places. Workers might only know how to use simple tools like Excel but not more advanced ones like Power BI, Tableau, or Python.

Many employees don't know enough about the company's critical data tools and how to use them. This makes it hard to do their jobs well. Workers often find it difficult to understand and use data correctly, so they can't always turn data into useful information. Technology changes fast, and the skills workers have can become old quickly. Without good training, it's hard to keep up. Companies might not have enough money or programs to teach their employees new data skills. Sometimes, training isn't available to everyone or isn't right for what each person needs to learn.

Talent Retention Issues

Hiring great data workers is only part of the challenge; keeping them is another big problem. The job market is very competitive, making it hard to hold on to skilled data professionals. Keeping top data workers is tough because other companies are also trying to hire them. Some companies offer higher salaries, making it hard to match competitors' pay. New or less-known companies might have difficulty attracting data talent compared to famous companies.

When workers leave soon after being hired, it hurts data projects and wastes time training them. If workers aren't happy or don't feel fulfilled in their jobs, they might leave. Skilled workers might find better jobs at other companies. Employees might leave if they don't see a clear path to growth in their jobs. Workers worry about not moving up in their careers. When it's not clear how to get promoted or what is expected, workers can feel lost and decide to leave.

Keeping talented data workers is important for a company's success. If employees feel happy, see opportunities to grow, and are treated well, they are more likely to stay and help the company use data to grow and succeed.

Resistance to New Roles and Responsibilities

Change can be scary. When companies add new data jobs or ask workers to do more tasks, some people might not like it. They might prefer doing the same things they always have. Sometimes, workers worry they won't learn the new skills or tools needed for these changes. They might also fear that new technology could replace their jobs. Adding more data work without giving them enough time can make them stressed and tired. This can lead to them not wanting to take on new tasks.

When companies give employees more work without the infrastructure or tools to make their jobs easier, it can cause problems. Workers might feel overwhelmed if they don't get the right help and clear instructions. Companies need to listen to their workers' worries and give them the training and tools they need to handle the changes.

Inadequate Engagement and Recognition

Keeping workers motivated is more than just giving them tasks. If workers don't see how data projects relate to their jobs or feel left out of decisions, they might not want to help with data work. Sometimes, workers don't feel excited or responsible for data projects because they don't understand their importance.

When there are few ways for workers to give feedback, or if their ideas are ignored, they can feel like their opinions don't matter. This can make them lose interest and avoid joining new projects. It's important for companies to listen to their workers and value their ideas.

Recognizing and celebrating workers' hard work is also very important. When companies praise their teams for their successes and efforts, workers feel good and want to keep helping. Showing appreciation for the data team's achievements can boost everyone's happiness and motivation.

Fixing these common challenges is key to helping your team work well with data. By understanding and solving these problems, you can build a happy, skilled, and ready team to help your company succeed with data.

Principle 1: Training and Education

Teaching your team new skills is very important. If they learn, they will find it easier to keep up with new things. Have you ever felt puzzled by big ideas like big data or machine learning? Your team might feel the same way.

By focusing on training and education, you help your team stay ahead. This principle has three parts: checking skills and helping them grow, teaching about data, and learning to handle changes. Let's look at the first part.

Skills Assessment and Development

Knowing what your team can do now is very important. You can only fix skill gap issues if you know where they begin. By checking their skills often, you can plan training that helps them and your company.

Have you ever tried to build something without the right tools? It can be hard, right? The same goes for your team. If they have the right skills, tasks can become manageable. Imagine if your team has the most relevant data tools and can use them easily to make smart daily choices. Would that help your company do better?

By making learning plans that match your business goals, everyone wins. Your team grows and learns new things, and your company moves closer to its goals. For example, if your company wants to use big data to understand what customers like, your team needs to know how to work with big data tools.

Actionable Steps for Assessing and Developing Skills

Conduct Comprehensive Skills Audits

Finding out where your team stands is the first step to getting better.

1. **Develop Simple Assessment Tools:** Create easy quizzes and tasks to see what skills people have. For example, ask if they know how to use tools like Power BI or Tableau, if they understand data privacy rules, or if they can write code in Python or SQL.
2. **Analyse Results to Identify Gaps:** After collecting answers, see where skills are missing. Many team members don't know about cloud storage or need to learn more about making charts and graphs.
3. **Prioritize Skills Based on Business Needs:** Focus on the most important skills for your company's goals. If your company

wants to use machine learning, then learning about that should come first.

Create Personalized Development Plans

Making special learning plans keeps your team excited and helps your business, a win-win.

1. **Align Individual Goals with Organizational Objectives:** Talk with each team member about what they want to learn and how it helps the company. This makes learning meaningful for everyone. For example, if someone wants to improve at data analysis, and your company needs that skill, it's a perfect match.
2. **Set Clear Learning Goals:** Make sure each person knows what they are aiming for and by when. For instance, someone might aim to learn how to use a new data tool in three months or complete an online course in data visualization.
3. **Provide Mentorship and Support:** Pair up team members so they can help each other. Someone good at using data tools can teach others. This not only helps them learn faster but also builds teamwork.

Allocate Resources Wisely

Putting time and money into training to make sure it works well.

1. **Invest in Relevant Training Programs:** Spend money on training that fills the skill gaps you find. These could be online courses, workshops, or bringing in experts to teach. For example, you could use learning platforms like Coursera, Pluralsight, or Udemy.
2. **Use Experts Inside Your Company:** Let team members who are good at certain skills teach others. This saves money and encourages sharing knowledge. It also makes your team feel valued for their expertise.
3. **Check Progress and Make Changes:** Keep an eye on how the training goes. Are people learning the skills they need? If not,

find out why and make changes. A different training method may work better.

These steps will make your team feel more valued and help your company reach its goals. When everyone is learning and improving, the whole team becomes stronger. A skilled team is like a well-oiled machine; it runs smoothly and gets the job done.

Data Literacy Initiatives

Data isn't just for the data team; it's for everyone in your company. When all your team members understand basic data concepts, they can make smarter choices and help build a data-driven culture. Think about it: Wouldn't meetings be better if everyone could understand the charts, numbers, and underlying concepts like averages and trends?

By teaching everyone about data, you ensure it's used all over your company, not just in one department. This helps different teams work together better because they speak the same language.

Actionable Steps for Improving Data Literacy

Launch Inclusive Training Programs

Making data learning easy to reach helps everyone get involved.

1. **Design a Comprehensive Curriculum:** Create lessons that cover basic data concepts for all employees. Topics could include understanding different kinds of data, simple math, making charts, and reading reports. Use examples from your own business to make it interesting.
2. **Offer Different Ways to Learn:** Some people like videos, while others like hands-on activities. Provide online courses, in-person classes, and fun group sessions. Have lunchtime talks where people can chat about data topics.

3. **Make Training Accessible:** Make sure everyone can join the training, regardless of their location or schedule. Use online platforms so people can learn when it's best for them.

Encourage Cross-Functional Participation

Getting everyone involved helps break down walls between departments.

1. **Work More Collaboratively:** Set up projects requiring different teams to work together using data. For example, in retail, warehouses and transportation could collaborate to find better ways to streamline their operations.
2. **Host Team Workshops:** Bring different teams together for data workshops. This helps people share what they know and learn from each other. Even better, if you're large enough, like Tesco, hold your own internal data conference.

Measure and Celebrate Progress

Recognizing achievements makes people want to keep going.

1. **Track Key Metrics:** Keep an eye on how much more people use data and make decisions with it. This could be counting how many data projects are done or how often data tools are used.
2. **Recognize Achievements:** Give a shout-out to teams and people who get better at using data. You could send an email, give awards, or other fun ways to say thanks.
3. **Gather Feedback and Refine Programs:** Find out what people think about the training. What's working well? What could be better? Use their ideas to make your data-learning programs even better.

These steps will help everyone in your company become more comfortable with data. This makes them better at their jobs and helps your company make smarter decisions. Remember, when everyone understands data, the whole company benefits.

Case Study: Lloyds Banking Group's Data Training Initiative

Lloyds Banking Group's £3 billion investment in people, technology, and data showcases their dedication to building strong data competencies across the company. They launched professional development programs for everyone, enhancing their data analytics skills and building a diverse team of experts and PhDs. This comprehensive approach highlights Lloyds' commitment to data-driven decision-making, aligning with its goal to leverage data and analytics for organizational success.

Adaptability Training

In the fast-changing world of data, adjusting is very important. New technologies emerge, new ways of doing things appear, and what worked yesterday might not work today. Have you thought about how your team handles change? Do they like new ideas or prefer to keep things the same? By helping your team become more adaptable, you ensure they stay good at their jobs and enjoy their work.

Developing adaptability means teaching them how to handle change, keeping up with new tools, and encouraging a flexible way of thinking. Imagine if your team could easily learn a new tool or adjust to a new process without any problems. This would help them and make your company stronger.

Actionable Steps for Adaptability Training

Provide Change Management Workshops

Helping your team understand and deal with change makes it less scary.

1. **Focus on Soft Skills:** Offer training in talking and listening, solving problems, and understanding others. These skills are

important when things change and help everyone work together better.
2. **Practice with Role-Playing:** Use scenarios and situations where teams have to handle changes, like using a new computer program or following new rules. This helps them get used to change safely.
3. **Continuous Support:** Give your team resources such as books or online materials so they can keep learning and growing, such as Coursera, Udemy, or PluralSights. Let them know you're there if they have any questions or need help.

Encourage Innovation

Letting your team try new things helps them become more adaptable and creative.

1. **Allocate Time for Experimentation**: Allow your team time to explore new ideas or technologies. This can lead to great new solutions and keep them excited about their work.
2. **Promote Collaborative Projects**: Encourage people from different teams to work together on projects. This helps them learn from each other and come up with new ideas.
3. **Reward Adaptability**: Recognize and celebrate team members who embrace change and think of new ways to do things. This makes others want to do the same.

Promote an Agile Mindset

An agile approach enables your team to respond quickly to new challenges.

1. **Implement Agile Methodologies:** Adopt agile practices like Scrum or Kanban in your project management. This encourages iterative development, regular feedback, and adaptability.
2. **Encourage Continuous Learning:** Build a culture where learning is valued and encouraged. Provide resources such as

subscriptions to professional journals, access to online courses, or attendance at industry conferences.

3. **Allocate Time for Innovation:** Allow employees dedicated time to explore new ideas or technologies. Google has a '20% time' initiative where, on top of their day-to-day job, employees are encouraged to spend 20% of their time working on what they think will most benefit Google. This can lead to innovative solutions and keep your team engaged.

By focusing on adaptability training, you're not just teaching new skills but building a strong team ready for the future. When you invest in your team's growth, they feel confident and can help move your data plans forward. Remember, tools and ways of working are important, but your people make the real difference.

Principle 2: Talent Management and Retention

Keeping your best people is very important. When you help your team grow and feel happy at work, they are more likely to stay. Have you ever had a teacher or coach who guided you and made you better? Companies need to do the same for their workers.

By focusing on talent management and making sure your team sees a bright future with you, your company becomes stronger. This principle has three parts: clear career paths, mentorship programs, and using team members who love data to inspire others.

Setting Clear Career Pathways

In a company, it's important for everyone to see where they can go next. Just like moving from one grade to another in school, employees feel happier when they know how they can move up their career ladder.

When your team sees a clear path ahead, they get excited and work harder.

Imagine showing your team how they can become leaders or experts. They could start as a Junior Data Analyst and become the Head of Data one day. Progressing through a clear path will help them feel valued and give them goals to reach for. When people know you care about their future, they are likelier to stay and do their best.

By providing clear and exciting career paths, you show your commitment to your team's growth. It helps match what they want with what the company needs. For example, if your company wants to use more data to make smarter choices, you can help your team gain the necessary experiences to move up.

Actionable Steps for Creating Career Pathways

Develop Career Frameworks

Creating a clear structure helps everyone understand how to grow in their roles.

1. **Map Out Roles and Levels**: Draw a picture or chart that shows all the jobs in your team, from beginners to leaders. For instance, someone might start as a Junior Data Analyst, then become a Senior Data Analyst, Lead Data Analyst, Analytics Manager, Senior Analytics Manager, Head of Data, and eventually, the Chief Data Officer.
2. **List Skills Needed for Each Step**: Write down what skills and knowledge are needed for each job level. This can include knowing how to use certain computer programs or being good at solving problems. For example, a Senior Data Analyst might need to be excellent at problem-solving and know advanced statistics and SQL.
3. **Share Career Paths with Everyone**: Make sure all team members know about these paths. You can have meetings, send

emails, or put up posters that show how they can grow in the company.

Support Career Development

Helping your team grow keeps them happy and committed.

1. **Provide Learning Resources**: Give your team chances to learn new skills. You can offer classes, workshops, or online courses. Websites like Coursera or Udemy have many lessons on data science. Helping them get certificates shows you care about their growth.
2. **Have Regular Career Talks**: Meet each team member to discuss their dreams and goals. Help them come up with a plan to get there. They may want to learn a new skill or work on a new project. These talks show you support them and want them to succeed.

By making clear and exciting career pathways, you help your team see a bright future working in your company. They will feel happier, work harder, and be more likely to stay. This not only helps them grow but also helps your company have a more stable team. When everyone knows they can move up and learn new things, it creates a happy and successful team.

Case Study: Verizon's Talent GPS – Clear Career Paths for Employees

Verizon, a big telecommunications company, saw that their employees needed better tools to grow their careers. In 2021, they launched Talent GPS, a tool that shows all the jobs available in the company and the skills needed for each job. Talent GPS is available to everyone, so all employees have the same chances to progress based on their skills and experiences.

Talent GPS also helps employees see the best ways to move up in the company by identifying their skill gaps and development areas. Verizon aims to use this tool to retain employees, make sure everyone has fair access to career information, and, overall, make employees happier and more involved in their work. Using Talent GPS, Verizon is helping its employees plan and build their future at the company.

Creating Mentorship Programs

Have you ever had someone more senior teach you something new? A teacher showed you how to solve a tricky math program, or a family taught you a fun game. In companies, mentors are like friendly guides who help others learn and grow. Mentorship programs let more experienced employees share their knowledge with newer team members. This allows everyone to get better at their jobs and increases job satisfaction for both parties, making them more likely to stay with the company longer.

When people feel supported and know they can learn from others, they become more excited about their work. Mentorship helps team members gain new skills, feel more confident, and become more integrated within the team.

Actionable Steps for Setting Up Mentorship Programs

Launch a Mentorship Initiative

Starting a mentorship program helps connect experienced and new team members.

1. **Identify Participants**: Find people who can be good mentors and those who want to learn. Mentors should be good at their jobs and enjoy helping others. Mentees are team members who want to grow and learn new things. For example, a skilled data expert can help a new worker who wants to learn about data.

2. **Set Clear Objectives**: Decide what you want the mentorship program to achieve. This could be learning new skills, helping people become leaders, or making teams work better together. Clear goals help everyone know what to expect.
3. **Provide Training for Mentors**: Teach mentors how to be great helpers. Show them how to listen carefully, give useful advice, and set goals with their mentees. Mentors can make a big difference when they know how to guide others.

Monitor and Evaluate the Program

Checking how the program is doing helps it stay effective.

1. **Collect Feedback**: Ask mentors and mentees how things are going. You can use surveys or have chats to hear their thoughts. This helps you understand what's working well and what might need to change.
2. **Adjust Accordingly**: If something isn't working, make changes. Mentors and mentees need more time together, or they may need extra resources. Keep improving the program so it stays useful for everyone.
3. **Celebrate Success**: When mentors and mentees achieve great things, share their stories! You can feature them in newsletters or give them special awards. This makes everyone feel proud and encourages others to join the program.

By creating a strong mentorship program, companies can help their workers learn new skills and feel happier at work. This means people are more likely to stay with the company and do their best. Mentorship also creates stronger bonds within the team by allowing everyone to support each other and grow together.

Case Study: Siemens' Data-Driven Mentoring Program

Siemens Building Technologies wanted to help employees grow and stay with the company. They started a mentoring program where experienced workers guided newer employees. With 7,500 employees, including 1,200 in the program, Siemens used data to check how well it worked. Anton Duvall, the CFO, looked at raises, promotions, and how many people left the company. He compared those with mentors to those without to ensure fair results.

The results were impressive. Employees with mentors were promoted 25% faster and got 35% higher salary increases. Managers in the program saw promotions 30% quicker and earned 61% more. Additionally, fewer mentored employees left Siemens, reducing turnover by three times. This data-driven mentoring program helped employees advance their careers and kept them happy and loyal, saving Siemens money and strengthening the company.

Leveraging Internal Champions

In a company, internal champions love using data and encourage others to do the same. These champions bridge the gap between leaders and the rest of the team, inspiring everyone to use data to make better decisions. By empowering these passionate employees, companies can quickly become more data-focused and make sure everyone uses data in their daily work.

Internal champions play a big role in making the company more data-driven. They show their teammates how data can solve problems and improve work. This helps everyone learn more about data and makes the whole company smarter and more efficient. When employees see their peers excited about data, it creates a positive environment where everyone wants to contribute and grow.

Actionable Steps for Internal Champions

Identify Data Enthusiasts

Finding employees who love working with data is the first step.

1. **Look for Passionate Employees**: Find employees who enjoy using data and talking about it in their work.
2. **Observe Their Work**: See who goes out of their way to use data in projects and who helps others with data tasks.
3. **Gather Recommendations**: Ask managers and team leaders to suggest employees who are great with data.

Empower Champions

Give these passionate employees the tools and support they need to lead.

1. **Provide Extra Resources**: Give champions access to special tools, training, or information to help them lead data projects.
2. **Offer Training and Development**: Help them learn more by providing additional training on advanced data topics or leadership skills.
3. **Create Leadership Opportunities**: Let them lead data initiatives or projects so they can use their skills to help the team.

Facilitate Peer Mentoring

Encourage champions to help others learn about data.

1. **Set Up Learning Groups**: Create small groups where champions can teach their peers about data.
2. **Organize Workshops**: Have champions run fun workshops where team members can learn new data skills together.
3. **Promote Sharing Success Stories**: Let champions share how they used data to solve problems, inspiring others to do the same.

By leveraging internal champions, companies can build a strong, data-loving team. These champions help everyone learn and use data better, making the company smarter and more successful. When employees see their peers using data to achieve great things, it creates a positive and motivated workplace where everyone works together to reach the company's goals.

Principle 3: Feedback and Recognition

Giving feedback and recognizing your team's effort and hard work are essential in building a motivated workplace where people will want to stay. When employees feel heard and appreciated, they are more excited to contribute their best ideas and participate in data initiatives. This principle ensures everyone is engaged, has ways to share their thoughts and ideas, and feels confident in using data to help the company succeed.

Getting Your Team Engaged

Getting your team involved is the key to making data projects successful. After all, they know their part of the business the best. When employees participate and feel they own the projects, everyone can share their ideas and work together to create great things with data. Inclusive decision-making means letting your team help plan and carry out data projects, which makes them feel more excited and committed.

Empowering employees by giving them the freedom to decide on data tasks can boost their motivation and productivity. Remember Google's '20% Time' initiative that I mentioned earlier in the chapter? Well, it led to new ideas like Gmail. Letting your team explore their ideas can bring amazing results.

Promoting open communication ensures that everyone feels comfortable sharing their thoughts and asking questions about data projects. Companies like Slack use special channels for data talks so everyone can share ideas and help each other. When your team communicates well, they work better together and develop smarter data solutions.

Actionable Steps for Employee Engagement

Facilitate Participation

Encouraging your team to take part helps everyone contribute to data projects.

1. **Create Cross-Functional Teams:** Mix people from different departments to work together on data projects. This helps everyone share their unique skills and ideas.
2. **Host Idea Workshops:** Hold meetings where employees can share their thoughts on using data. These can be brainstorming sessions or hackathons.
3. **Support Initiatives:** Help employees start their own data projects by providing the necessary tools and guidance. This makes them feel responsible and proud of their work.

Enhance Communication

Good communication keeps everyone informed and allows ideas to flow freely.

1. **Regular Briefings:** Keep everyone updated on how data projects are going. Share progress and changes with simple updates like newsletters or short videos.
2. **Utilize Digital Platforms:** Use tools like Microsoft Teams or Slack to make it easy for your team to talk and share ideas about data projects anytime, anywhere.
3. **Feedback Sessions:** Create chances for employees to share their thoughts and suggestions about data projects. This can be through meetings, surveys, or one-on-one talks.

These steps ensure your team feels involved and valued in data projects. When everyone is engaged and communicates well, your data initiatives will be stronger and more successful. This helps build a positive, lasting culture where data drives the company forward.

Setting Feedback Mechanisms

Having ways for your team to share their thoughts and ideas is important. When employees have the channel to give feedback, it helps discover meaningful projects, including data initiatives. Good feedback mechanisms allow people to talk to each other, surface good ideas, and show that their ideas matter.

For example, IBM has programs where younger employees teach more senior teams about new data trends, ensuring everyone understands and feels valued. Amazon uses a 'Working Backwards' method, where employees think about what customers need and use that to guide data projects. Google lets employees suggest ways to improve tools, and the best ideas are used and rewarded. These programs help everyone feel like they are part of making data work well for the company.

Actionable Steps for Feedback Mechanisms

Implement Feedback Tools

Using the right tools makes it easy for everyone to share their ideas and opinions.

1. **Use Surveys and Polls:** Ask employees regularly what they think by using surveys. Tools like SurveyMonkey or Qualtrics can help gather everyone's opinions.
2. **Set Up Suggestion Boxes:** Provide both physical and online boxes where employees can anonymously share their ideas. This is great for getting honest feedback on sensitive topics.

3. **Create Digital Forums:** Use platforms like Slack or Microsoft Teams to have special places where employees can give real-time feedback on data projects.

Act on Feedback

Acting on feedback shows that you value what your team says and helps improve data projects.

1. **Look at the Answers:** Use tools to find common ideas and important issues from the feedback. This helps you know what to focus on.
2. **Share the Changes:** Let everyone know what changes are being made because of their feedback through emails, posts, or meetings. This shows that their input is making a difference.
3. **Close the Loop:** Ensure employees see how their ideas have helped by sharing updates on how their suggestions are being used. This can be done through special campaigns or progress dashboards.

Setting up these feedback mechanisms lets your company improve its data projects and keeps your team happy and involved. When employees know their voices are heard, and their ideas are used, they feel more connected and motivated to help the company succeed with data.

Case Study: Microsoft's AI-Driven Survey Initiative

Microsoft developed 'Pulse Surveys', an AI-driven initiative that automatically analyses real-time responses from employees. This allows executives to quickly address concerns and make data-informed decisions about workplace culture in a transparent manner, a quick win for the business.

By addressing common barriers and implementing these strategies early, you can help your company embrace a data-driven mindset more smoothly. A proactive approach alleviates concerns and lays the groundwork for a more resilient and innovative data-driven culture. Engage your employees through transparent communication, provide proper resources, and celebrate early wins to ensure your company moves in the right direction on its data maturity journey.

Building Confidence in Data

When people see how data has helped others, they feel more certain about using it themselves. Sharing stories of success shows that using data works and makes others want to try it, too.

When your team trusts that data can help them do their jobs better, they get more excited about using it. Confidence grows when they see real examples of data making a positive difference. For instance, if the sales team uses data to understand what customers like and sees their sales increase, other teams might think, 'Maybe data can help us too!'

Building confidence turns data from something that might seem hard or confusing into a helpful tool everyone wants to use. It helps your whole company improve at making smart decisions and encourages everyone to keep learning and improving.

Actionable Steps for Building Confidence

Publicize Data-Driven Achievements

Showing how data has helped can inspire others to use data too.

1. **Share Success Stories:** Tell everyone about times when using data led to good results. For example, explain how the customer service team used data to answer questions faster or how the marketing team used data to reach more people.
2. **Use Real Examples:** Provide actual numbers or facts to show the impact of data. This makes the benefits clear and believable. For instance, 'After using data to plan our deliveries, we saved 20% on fuel costs!'

3. **Celebrate Wins:** Hold meetings or send messages to praise teams who used data successfully. This makes everyone feel proud and shows that using data is important to the company.

Recognize Contributions

Thanking those who use data well encourages them and others.

1. **Acknowledge Teams and Individuals:** Give shout-outs to people who did a great job using data. Say things like, 'Great job to Alex for using data to improve our website's conversion rate!'
2. **Awards and Rewards:** Offer small prizes or certificates to recognize their hard work. Maybe have a 'Data Hero' award each month.
3. **Public Recognition:** Share their success stories in company newsletters or team meetings. This makes them feel good and encourages others to follow their example.

Encourage Knowledge Sharing

Helping everyone learn from each other makes the whole team better with data.

1. **Create Learning Groups:** Set up times for people to share what they've learned about using data. They can have lunch-and-learn sessions or workshops where they teach each other.
2. **Share Best Practices:** Let people show others the best ways to use data tools. For example, someone good at making charts can teach others how to do it.
3. **Support Collaboration:** Encourage teams to work together on data projects and share what they discover. This builds teamwork and helps spread confidence in using data.

By doing these things, you help your team feel more confident about using data. When people see real benefits and feel appreciated, they are more likely to use data in their work. This builds a strong culture where data helps everyone succeed.

Case Study: Network Rail's Gold Award for Data-Driven Dashboard

Network Rail's £335m seven-year transformation programme aims to use data to improve the UK's rail network. I worked on an initiative where we created a decision support dashboard for the maintenance team, which involved a lot of heavy data analytics. This dashboard helped them make better decisions quickly. It saved a lot of money and made the maintenance work more efficient. By using data that everyone could access and understand, we made maintenance easier and showed how important data is.

Because the dashboard was so successful, our team was recognized and won a gold award in the transformation program. This award showed how much our project helped Network Rail. It proved that using smart data tools can make a big difference, helping the company make better decisions and succeed in the long run.

Summary

'People' is an important component of building a data-driven company. Overall, we discussed 1) training and education, 2) talent management and retention, and 3) feedback and recognition. Each one helps your team learn, stay happy, and use data to make smart choices.

Firstly, training and education make sure your team has the right skills. By teaching them new things and helping them grow, they can handle big ideas like big data and machine learning. This allows everyone to work better and reach the company's goals.

Secondly, talent management and retention keep your best people happy and eager to stay. Clear career paths, good mentors, and recognizing those who love data make your team feel valued. This makes your team strong and loyal.

Lastly, feedback and recognition ensure your team feels heard and appreciated. When you listen to their ideas and celebrate their successes, they become more motivated to use data. This builds confidence and a positive culture where data helps everyone succeed.

By focusing on these three principles, you create a happy and skilled team that uses data to help your company grow and thrive.

Chapter 6:
Developing Effective Processes

In this chapter, we'll explore the 'process' component, which is step 4 of our data strategy framework. This step is about setting up best practices to manage your data effectively.

As we've talked about before, data is very valuable. It can help you grow, think of new ideas, and stay ahead of your competition. But just having lots of data is just the beginning; it's not enough. The real power of data comes when we have strong data governance, which is a set of rules and methods to ensure we handle data properly across the company.

Good data governance shapes how we take care of and use our data. It turns scattered efforts into organised actions that fit your business goals, making sure your data is reliable, easy to access, and used correctly.

Defining Data Governance and Processes

The fundamentals of data governance cover these key elements:

1. **Standardisation of Data Practices**: Establishing consistent methods for collecting, storing, and using data. This standardisation ensures your team can understand and work with the data seamlessly, reducing errors and improving efficiency.
2. **Clear Roles and Responsibilities**: Defining who is responsible for various data-related tasks. This includes appointing data stewards and setting up accountability structures to maintain data quality and integrity.
3. **Compliance and Ethical Use**: Ensuring all data activities follow legal regulations and ethical standards. This involves creating data policies that protect privacy, secure sensitive information, and build trust with customers and stakeholders.
4. **Aligning Data Initiatives with Business Goals**: Connecting data projects directly to your business objectives ensures that your efforts are strategic and impactful. It transforms data initiatives from isolated tasks into integral parts of your business plan.
5. **Supporting Innovation and Growth**: Providing a secure and well-managed data environment allows teams to explore new ideas confidently. Clear guidelines and reliable data empower you to leverage information innovatively, driving continuous improvement and adaptability.

The Role and Importance of Data Governance and Processes

Data governance and processes are vital parts of your data strategy. They form the foundation for managing data as a strategic asset. With effective data governance, we ensure consistency across the organisation. It creates a single source of truth. This means all departments use data in the same way, which reduces confusion and mistakes.

Data governance also helps align your data projects with the business goals. Doing this ensures that your data efforts support key priorities and have a real impact.

Proper governance reduces risks like data breaches, breaking laws, and poor data quality. It helps you follow regulations and avoid legal problems. It also protects sensitive information from unauthorised access.

Having standardised processes improves how we work. It streamlines workflows, reduces unnecessary tasks, and boosts teamwork across different teams. This efficiency leads to better decision-making because choices are based on accurate and reliable data.

In short, data governance and processes are essential. They turn your data into a powerful tool that supports your goals, keeps you safe from risks, and makes your operations run smoothly.

Common Challenges

Like other components we've discussed so far, implementing robust data governance and processes isn't straightforward. Companies encounter obstacles that can slow down or even halt their progress. Recognising these challenges is the first step toward overcoming them.

Lack of Standardisation

One major hurdle is the lack of standardisation. Imagine if everyone in your company used different measurements, some using inches, others using centimetres. It would create confusion, right? Similarly, when different departments use varied data formats, it becomes difficult to integrate and analyse information effectively.

Inconsistent data formats mean one team might record dates as 'Day/Month/Year,' while another uses 'Month/Day/Year.' This inconsistency can lead to errors when combining data. Varied definitions of key terms add to the confusion. For instance, aligning data and implementing impactful data initiatives becomes challenging if one part of the business starts its week on a Sunday and other parts start on a Monday. Siloed processes, where departments handle data independently without coordination, further hinder a unified approach to data management.

Undefined Roles and Responsibilities

Another significant challenge is not having clear roles and responsibilities regarding data. Important data problems may go unaddressed if it's unclear who is accountable for data quality or governance tasks. This ambiguity can result in data errors persisting because everyone assumes someone else is handling them.

Overlapping duties can also waste time and resources. Multiple people might unknowingly duplicate efforts, leading to inefficiency. Without designated data stewards or clear accountability structures, there's a lack of ownership. Like the above, data problems might not be promptly resolved, impacting decision-making and overall efficiency.

We can proactively address these challenges by understanding and acknowledging them. Establishing standard practices and clearly defining roles helps build a solid foundation for effective data governance, ultimately supporting your organisation's goals and success.

Poor Data Quality Management

Another significant challenge is poor data quality management. Think of your company's data as a garden. If you neglect this garden, weeds grow, and plants wither. Similarly, ignoring data quality leads to serious problems.

Data errors and inaccuracies are like rotten vegetables mixed with fresh ones. When decision-makers rely on faulty information, it's like cooking with bad ingredients; the results can be disastrous. For example, incorrect customer addresses could result in missed deliveries and unhappy clients.

Outdated information is akin to forgetting to water your plants. Without regular updates, your data becomes stale and useless. It's like trying to plan this year's harvest based on weather data from 10 years ago.

Inadequate validation processes are like not checking for pests before introducing new plants to your garden. Bad data can enter your systems unchecked and spread without proper checks, causing widespread issues.

Compliance and Ethical Issues

Compliance and ethical issues present another set of challenges. These are like the rules of being a good neighbour in your data garden.

Regulatory non-compliance is like using banned pesticides in your garden. Laws like GDPR dictate how you should handle certain types of data. Ignoring these regulations can have severe consequences, including hefty fines and legal troubles.

Ethical missteps are similar to trampling on your neighbour's prized roses. Mishandling sensitive data can seriously damage your reputation and break the trust of your customers and partners. For instance, using personal data without consent can lead to backlash and loss of business.

Privacy concerns are about protecting the fences around your data garden. If you don't have strong security measures, it's like leaving your gate wide open. Personal information could be stolen, leading to data breaches that harm your customers and business.

By understanding these challenges, we can take steps to address them, ensuring your data remains a valuable and well-tended asset that supports your company's growth and integrity.

Principle 1: Data Governance Principles

Effective data governance is the foundation of a successful data strategy. It establishes the rules and processes that ensure data is managed consistently and responsibly across the organisation. By implementing robust data governance principles, organisations can enhance data quality, ensure compliance with regulations, and foster a culture where data is trusted and effectively utilised for decision-making.

Standardising Data Practices

Standardisation means ensuring everyone in the company uses data in the same way. It's like everyone agreeing to use the same words and rules so we all understand each other. This makes working together easier and helps you make better decisions.

For example, let's say we have a 'Product ID' for things we sell. If every part of the company uses the same kind of 'Product ID', then sharing information is simple. However, this is not always the case, especially in larger companies where individual departments will have their own IDs. We can create a unified data model, like a big visual plan showing how all your data fits together.

We can also make a data dictionary. This is a list that explains what important words mean. For instance, 'Active Customer' might mean someone who bought something in the last year. When everyone uses the same definitions, there's less confusion.

Having standard processes is important, too. This means we collect, store, and find data in the same way every time. For example, we follow the same steps when we add a new customer's information. This keeps your data neat and easy to use.

Actionable Steps for Standardisation:

Develop Data Standards Documentation

To achieve standardisation, begin by developing thorough documentation of data standards. This serves as a reference for all employees and promotes consistency in data handling.

1. **Create a Data Dictionary:** Compile definitions and formats for all critical data elements. This document should be accessible to all employees and regularly updated to reflect changes.
2. **Establish Data Modelling Standards:** Define how data is structured and related. This could involve setting guidelines for database schemas or data warehouse designs to ensure consistency.
3. **Implement Standard Operating Procedures (SOPs):** Document and disseminate processes for data handling. SOPs should provide clear data entry, validation, storage, and retrieval instructions.

Facilitate Cross-Department Collaboration

Collaboration across departments ensures that data standards are practical and adopted organisation-wide. This fosters a unified approach to data management.

1. **Form a Data Governance Committee:** Include representatives from key departments such as IT, finance, marketing, and operations. This committee oversees the development and enforcement of data standards.
2. **Regular Meetings:** Schedule ongoing sessions to review and update standards. Regular interaction ensures that data governance remains aligned with organisational goals and addresses any emerging issues.
3. **Feedback Mechanisms:** Allow for input from various stakeholders to refine standards. Implement channels like suggestion boxes or online forums where employees can provide feedback or report inconsistencies.

Organisations create a solid foundation for effective data governance by focusing on standardisation. This leads to more reliable data, better decision-making, and a stronger alignment with business objectives.

Case Study: Uber's Data Quality Standardization Initiative

Uber implemented a comprehensive data quality standardisation initiative to ensure the reliability and accuracy of their extensive data ecosystem. They developed the Uber Data Quality (UDQ) platform, which monitors and automatically detects data quality issues across the organisation. This platform supports over 2,000 critical datasets and has successfully identified around 90% of data quality incidents.

By standardising data practices, Uber significantly improved their decision-making processes with reliable and accurate data. The initiative also reduced the need for manual efforts in investigating and fixing poor data, enhancing operational efficiency. Additionally, UDQ prevented unnoticed data degradations that could lead to inconsistent behaviours, ensuring smooth and dependable operations.

Uber's data quality standardisation has made its data-driven operations more trustworthy and efficient, enabling better business decisions and supporting the company's growth and success.

Setting Data Policies

Data policies are like the rules of a game that everyone in the company follows when using information. They help you know how to use, share, and take care of data properly, much like traffic laws keep drivers safe on the road. By having clear data policies, everyone understands what they can and cannot do, which makes the company run smoothly and keeps important information safe.

One key part of data policies is usage guidelines. These guidelines tell you who can see and use different kinds of data. For example, only the teachers can access the student's test scores in a school, while the principal can see all the class's results. By knowing who can access what information, you make sure that data is used correctly and kept safe from people who shouldn't see it.

Another important part is sharing protocols. These are the rules about how you share data with others, both inside and outside the company. It's like knowing when to share a secret with a friend and when to keep it to yourself. For instance, you might be allowed to share how many products were sold with your marketing team, but you should keep customers' personal details private from people outside the company. Following these rules helps protect everyone's privacy and keeps the company trustworthy.

Data retention schedules tell you how long it takes to keep different kinds of data before deleting them. Just like you might keep your school assignments for the whole year but throw away old snack wrappers daily, companies decide how long to keep information. For example, keep important financial records for seven years but delete old emails after one year. This helps you manage your storage space and ensures you're not holding onto unnecessary information.

By understanding and following data policies, everyone in the company knows how to handle information responsibly. This keeps your data safe and helps you work together better. When everyone follows the same rules, you avoid mistakes, protect people's privacy, and make sure your company stays strong and trusted by others.

Actionable Steps for Setting Rules For Data Use

Create Comprehensive Data Policies

It's essential to write down clear and detailed rules to ensure everyone in your company knows how to handle data correctly. These comprehensive data policies guide all employees, helping them understand their responsibilities and the correct procedures to follow.

1. **Access Control Policies:** Decide who can access different areas of the database and write these rules down clearly. For instance, only the finance team can see financial reports, while all employees can access the company calendar.
2. **Data Sharing Agreements:** Set rules for sharing data with others. This includes how you share data within the company and with outside partners. For example, you might require approval from a manager before sharing data externally.
3. **Data Retention Policies:** Establish how long you keep different kinds of data. For example, customer inquiries might be kept for one year, while legal documents are kept for ten years.

Communicate Policies Organization-Wide

Once your data policies are created, it's important to make sure everyone in your company knows about them and understands what they mean. Strong communication ensures that all team members are on the same page and can follow the policies correctly.

1. **Policy Training Sessions**: Hold meetings or workshops to teach everyone about data policies. You can use examples and stories to make learning fun and easy to remember.
2. **Accessible Documentation**: Make the data policies easy to find, like putting them on the company intranet or in a handbook everyone can access. This way, people can check the rules whenever they need to.
3. **Acknowledge Receipt and Understanding**: Ask everyone to sign a form or click a button to confirm they have read and understand the policies. This helps make sure that everyone is aware of the rules.

Creating clear data policies and sharing them with everyone, you help your company use data responsibly and safely. This keeps your information secure and helps your team work better together. Following these steps ensures everyone knows the rules and can do their best work without confusion.

Ensuring Compliance and Ethics

Compliance and ethics in data governance are like the safety rules you follow when riding a bike. They help keep you on the right path and protect you from getting hurt. By following these rules, your company makes sure it uses data correctly, keeps everyone's information safe, and stays out of trouble with the law.

Regulatory compliance means following the laws about using and handling data. For example, laws like the GDPR in Europe or the CCPA in California tell you how to collect, use, and store people's personal information. These laws might require you to get permission before collecting someone's data and let them ask you to delete it if they want.

Ethical standards go beyond just following the law. They are about doing the right thing with data, even when no one is watching. This means being fair and honest, not using data to harm others, and ensuring your actions help people. For example, if you're using a computer program to make decisions, you should check that it's not unfairly treating some people differently than others.

Protecting privacy is a big part of both compliance and ethics. This means keeping people's personal information safe from those who shouldn't see it. You can do this by using special tools like locks on the data, hiding people's names, or making sure only the right people can access certain information.

Focusing on compliance and ethics helps your company build trust with customers and avoid problems. It's about more than what you can do with data; it's what you should do to be responsible and fair.

Actionable Steps for Ensuring Compliance and Ethics

Implement Compliance Monitoring Systems

To make sure you're always following the rules and acting ethically, it's important to have processes that regularly check how you handle data. These systems help you catch any issues early on and show others that you take compliance seriously.

1. **Regulatory Audits**: Conduct regular checks to ensure you follow laws like GDPR and CCPA. This might include reviewing how you collect data, how you get permission, and how long you keep data.

2. **Ethics Committees**: Create a group of people who look at data projects to ensure they are fair and good. They can help you decide if a new idea is okay or might cause problems.
3. **Privacy Impact Assessments**: Evaluate how your data practices affect people's privacy. This enables you to find and fix any issues before they become bigger problems.

Provide Compliance Training

Educating everyone in your company about the importance of compliance and ethics ensures that all team members know how to handle data properly. This shared understanding helps prevent mistakes and promotes a culture of responsibility.

1. **Legal Workshops**: Offer classes on data protection laws so everyone knows what to follow.
2. **Ethics Training**: Educate employees on using data responsibly and what to do if they face tricky situations.
3. **Certification Programs**: Encourage your team to get special certificates in data compliance to show they understand and can handle data properly.

By taking these steps, you ensure that your company handles data in a legal and ethical way. This protects your business from potential problems and builds trust with your customers and partners. When everyone knows the rules and understands why they matter, your company can use data confidently and responsibly.

Principle 2: Roles and Responsibilities

Knowing who does what is very important in any team. If people aren't sure about their jobs, things can get confusing. Have you ever been in a group where no one knows who should do a task? It can cause problems and slow everything down.

By clearly defining roles and responsibilities, everyone knows what they should do. This helps the team work better and reach goals faster. This principle has three parts: Data Stewardship, Clear Definitions, and Accountability Structures. Let's start with the first part.

Data Stewardship

Data stewardship is like having designated helpers who take care of your company's data. They make sure the data is good, clean, and useful. They are like gardeners who look after plants in a garden, making sure everything grows well.

These data stewards are normally responsible for their designated areas. For example, one person might take care of all the customer information, while another looks after product details. They know more about their data area and help others understand it.

It's important for everyone to feel responsible for the data they use. For example, in a family where everyone helps keep the house tidy, in a company, everyone should help keep the data in good shape. Data stewards lead the way by teaching others and showing how to handle data properly.

One big job of data stewards is making sure the data is correct. They check the data regularly, fix mistakes, and ensure its reliability. This helps the company make good decisions based on accurate information.

Actionable Steps in Deciding Who Manages the Data

Define Data Steward Roles

Firstly, choosing the right people and clearly explaining their responsibilities is important. This helps everyone know what to do and who to go to for help.

1. **Create Clear Job Descriptions:** Write down what each data steward should do. This might include taking care of certain data, checking its quality, and helping others understand it.
2. **Select the Right People:** Pick employees who are knowledgeable about their area and enjoy working with data. They should be good at explaining things to others.
3. **Give Them Authority:** Make sure data stewards have the power to make decisions about the data. They should be able to fix problems and set rules.

Establish Stewardship Programs

Next, set up programs to support your data stewards. This helps them learn and do their jobs better.

1. **Provide Training and Education:** Teach data stewards how to manage and keep data clean and useful.
2. **Hold Regular Meetings:** Let data stewards discuss challenges and share ideas. This helps everyone learn new things.
3. **Recognise Their Efforts:** Thank data stewards who do a good job. You can give them awards or special mentions.

Encourage Teamwork Across Departments

When different teams work together on data, it becomes more valuable for everyone.

1. **Hold Group Meetings:** Bring people from different business areas together to discuss data. They can share what they know and learn from each other.
2. **Share Good Ideas:** If one team has a smart way of handling data, let others know. Sharing tips helps everyone improve.
3. **Set Common Rules:** Work with all the teams to decide how data should be collected and stored. Having the same rules makes it easier for everyone to use the data.

Enhancing these steps will create a strong foundation for data stewardship in your company. This means better data quality, smarter decisions, and a team that works well together to keep your data valuable and reliable. Remember, taking good care of data is like caring for a garden, it needs attention and teamwork to flourish.

Clear Roles & Responsibilities

Clear definitions of roles and responsibilities in data governance are like assigning positions in a sports team. Each player needs to know their specific role to work together effectively and avoid confusion on the field.

Role clarity is crucial in data processes. This means clearly defining who does what, much like how a quarterback has different responsibilities than a wide receiver in football. For example, a Data Quality Analyst might monitor data accuracy, while a Data Security Officer focuses on protecting sensitive information.

A responsibility assignment matrix, often called a RACI chart, is useful for mapping out roles. RACI stands for Responsible (the doer), Accountable (the ultimate decision-maker), Consulted (provides input), and Informed (kept in the loop). This chart clearly shows who's in charge of each task, who needs to approve decisions, who should be consulted for input, and who needs to be kept in the loop. For instance, in a data quality initiative, the data steward might be 'responsible' for implementing quality checks, the Chief Data Officer is 'accountable' for the overall success, the IT teams are 'consulted' on technical aspects, and department heads are 'informed' of progress.

Organisational alignment ensures that data governance roles fit seamlessly into the company's structure and support its goals. This is like making sure your football team's lineup matches your overall game strategy. For example, if a company prioritises customer experience, they might create a specific role for a Customer Data Steward who works closely with the customer service department.

Actionable Steps in Roles & Responsibilities

Develop a Governance Structure Chart

Creating a clear structure helps everyone see how roles fit together.

1. **Create Visual Diagrams:** Draw pictures showing how different data roles connect to each other and the rest of the company. This could be like an organisational chart for data governance.
2. **Write Detailed Job Descriptions:** Describe each role clearly, including what they do, the skills they need, and how they help with data governance. Keep these descriptions where everyone can easily find them, like a shared online folder.
3. **Get Leadership Approval:** Show the structure chart to company leaders and get their agreement. This helps ensure everyone supports the defined roles and understands their importance.

Communicate Roles and Responsibilities

Making sure everyone knows their roles helps the team work smoothly.

1. **Hold Orientation Sessions:** Teach all employees about the data governance framework during new employee orientations and regular training sessions. This helps everyone understand how data is managed in the company.
2. **Regularly Update Roles:** As the company grows or changes, update the roles to fit new needs. For example, if new laws come in, you might need a new role focused on compliance. Let everyone know about these changes right away.
3. **Set Up Feedback Channels:** Create ways for employees to share their thoughts on how roles work. This could be through

surveys, suggestion boxes, or regular meetings where people can speak up about what's working and what's not.

Implement a Responsibility Assignment Matrix

Using the Responsibility Assignment Matrix RACI Charts. This approach makes it easy to see who is in charge of what, so there's no confusion or overlap.

1. **Create a RACI Chart:** Write down all the data governance tasks, then note who is responsible, accountable, consulted, and informed for each one of them. This clear outline ensures everyone understands their duties.
2. **Review and Update Regularly:** As your company changes, so do responsibilities. Check the RACI chart often to ensure it still fits your current team structure and projects, making updates as needed.
3. **Train Employees on Using the Matrix:** Teach everyone how to read and use the RACI chart. This ensures everyone understands their roles and how they fit into the bigger picture.

Organisations can create a more efficient and effective data governance structure by clearly defining and communicating roles and responsibilities. This clarity helps prevent duplication of efforts, ensures all necessary tasks are covered, and allows for better collaboration across the organisation. Remember, just like in sports, a well-coordinated team with clear roles is more likely to succeed in achieving its goals.

Case Study: Macmillan Cancer Support's Keeping Data Safe Framework

Macmillan Cancer Support introduced the Keeping Data Safe (KDS) framework to enhance data protection and governance. They created three specialised groups: Keeping Data Safe groups, Senior Responsible Owners (SROs), and Data Protection Managers. This structure ensured each team had clear roles and responsibilities for safely managing data.

SROs took ownership of residual data protection risks, while Data Protection Managers oversaw daily data security tasks. The hierarchical setup improved involvement from senior leaders, making data protection a priority across the organisation. Additionally, a clear escalation path for the Data Protection Officer (DPO) ensured that issues were promptly addressed.

As a result, Macmillan minimised data protection risks, improved governance, and increased accountability among employees. The KDS framework led to better data management practices, safeguarding sensitive information and strengthening the organisation's overall security.

Accountability Structure

Similar to the above, accountability structures in data governance are like the rules of a game that ensure everyone plays their part correctly. These structures help everyone understand their responsibilities and ensure that data is kept safe and accurate.

Performance metrics are like scoreboards showing how well everyone does their data tasks. By including data governance in job reviews, companies show that taking care of data is very important. For example, a data steward might be checked on how accurate the data is or how quickly they fix data mistakes. This ensures that data governance is a key part of everyone's job.

Regular reporting on data management activities is like keeping a diary of how data is handled. These reports, done monthly or quarterly, show how good the data is, any data problems, or how data projects are going. These reports help everyone see how well the data is managed and how long it takes to fix problems.

Issue resolution processes are like planning what to do when something goes wrong with the data. The team might fix small problems, while bigger issues go to managers or a special committee. This helps ensure data rules are followed, and problems are fixed immediately.

Actionable Steps for Accountability Structures

Integrate Data Governance into KPIs

Making data tasks part of performance goals helps everyone take data seriously.

1. **Set Measurable Goals:** Create clear goals like reducing data errors by half in six months or making sure all sensitive data is protected. These goals give everyone something to aim for and show what success looks like.
2. **Conduct Regular Reviews:** Check how well people meet these goals during job reviews or special data check-ins. This helps see who is doing well and who might need extra help or training.
3. **Offer Rewards for Success:** Give rewards like bonuses, certificates, or special recognition to those who meet or exceed their data goals. This encourages everyone to work hard on data governance and feel proud of their achievements.

Develop Regular Reporting Systems

Keeping track of data management with regular reports ensures everyone knows how things are going.

1. **Create Simple Report Templates:** Make easy-to-use forms for people to fill out about their data tasks. This helps collect consistent information every time and makes reporting easier for everyone.
2. **Schedule Regular Report Times:** Decide when reports should be done every month or quarter. This keeps everyone on track and spots problems early before they get bigger.

3. **Share Reports with Everyone:** Make sure all team members can see the reports so they know how data is being handled. This transparency helps everyone stay informed and work together to improve data management.

Implement Issue Resolution Procedures

Having clear steps for fixing data problems keeps everything running smoothly.

1. **Define the Steps for Fixing Problems:** Write down what to do when a data issue happens, starting from who to tell first to how to solve the problem. This makes sure everyone knows what to do.
2. **Train Everyone on the Procedures:** Teach all team members to follow a list of steps when there is a data problem. This ensures everyone is prepared and knows their role in fixing issues.
3. **Review and Improve the Procedures:** Regularly review how well the problem-solving process works and make changes if needed. This keeps the process effective and helps prevent future problems.

By putting these accountability structures in place, your company can make sure data governance is a strong and important part of everyone's job. This keeps your data safe and reliable, helps your team work better together, and makes your company successful. Remember, when everyone is responsible for their part, the whole team can reach its goals.

Principle 3: Data Quality and Management

Keeping your data clean and well-organised is super important. Good data helps your team make smart decisions and keeps everything running smoothly. Let's dive into how you can make sure your data is always top-notch.

Ensuring Data Quality

Making sure your data is good and reliable is very important. If your data is wrong or messy, it can lead to bad decisions and cause problems. To ensure data quality, you need to set rules that help you know if your data is good. These rules make sure your data is correct, complete, and up-to-date. When your data meets these standards, it's useful for everyone.

Think of data quality like building a strong house. If the bricks (your data) are strong and well-placed, the house (your company) will stand firm. To set strong quality standards, focus on important things like:

1. **Accuracy**: Make sure the data is correct. For example, check that customer addresses match postal records. Imagine sending a letter to the wrong address, it wouldn't reach your friend!
2. **Completeness**: All the needed information should be there. A customer's record should have their name, contact info, and purchase history. It's like having all the puzzle pieces to see the full picture.
3. **Timeliness**: Data should be current and ready when you need it. For example, inventory information should be updated frequently enough to ensure everything stays in stock. Just like fresh bread tastes best, fresh data is most useful.
4. **Consistency**: Data should look the same everywhere. Use the same date format in all your systems, like MM/DD/YYYY.

Think how confusing it would be if clocks showed different times!
5. **Validity**: Data should follow the right rules and be in the correct format. For example, a birth date shouldn't be set in the future.

To keep these standards high, you can look for mistakes or duplicates, ensure data follows your business needs, and check data against trusted sources for accuracy.

Actionable Steps for Setting Data Quality Standards

Create Clear Data Quality Guidelines

Having clear rules helps everyone to know what is expected.

1. **Write Down What Good Data Is:** Decide what good data means for your team. Should all names have a first and last name? Should numbers be within a certain range? Write these rules down so everyone knows. For example, you might specify that phone numbers must have ten digits.
2. **Make Checklists to Review Data:** Create simple lists that help people check if the data meets the rules. This makes it easier to spot mistakes. Team members can use these checklists when entering or reviewing data.
3. **Choose a Team to Watch Over Data:** Pick some people who will be in charge of making sure the data stays good. They can help others follow the rules and answer questions about data quality.

Use Tools to Check Your Data

Invest in software that'll help you find and fix mistakes faster.

1. **Use Software to Find Errors**: These programs can spot missing information or numbers that don't make sense by looking at trends and anomalies. For example, we normally sell 100 products per day, but one day, we sold 1000 per day for no

clear reason. There are lots of solutions and tools that can pick this up.

2. **Do Regular Checks by Hand:** Sometimes, it's good to have people look over the data to catch mistakes that computers might miss, schedule times for team members to review data entries for accuracy.
3. **Let Everyone Report Mistakes:** Make it easy for anyone to say if they find a problem with the data. This way, mistakes can be fixed quickly. You could have a simple form or email where people can report issues.

Establish Data Quality Metrics

Knowing how good your data is helps you improve.

1. **Define Key Metrics**: Decide what numbers you'll track, like the percentage of data recorded without errors or the time it takes to correct mistakes. This is exactly what we did in one of my recent projects.
2. **Regular Reporting**: Create reports that show these metrics over time to see how you're doing. Share these reports with the team to keep everyone informed.
3. **Set Improvement Goals**: Aim to improve your metrics by a certain amount each month or quarter. Celebrate when you reach these goals to motivate the team.

By following these steps, you can ensure your data is accurate and helpful. Good data helps everyone make better decisions and keeps your company running smoothly.

Case Study: Network Rail's Data Governance & Quality Dashboard

Network Rail developed their first-ever Data Governance & Quality Dashboard to pinpoint data quality issues across various disciplines and regions. This tool helps senior stakeholders secure more resources to address data problems effectively. Additionally, it unlocks benefits for multiple ongoing data initiatives that depend on these data sources. By implementing this dashboard, Network Rail ensures that data quality is continuously improved and maintained, supporting better decision-making and enhancing the success of their data projects.

Data Integrity Guidelines

Keeping your data safe and unaltered is very important. Data integrity means making sure your data stays the same from the moment it's created until it's used. It's like keeping a treasure chest locked so no one can take or change what's inside without permission.

While data quality is about having accurate and complete data, data integrity focuses on protecting your data from being changed accidentally or by people who shouldn't. This ensures that the information you rely on is trustworthy.

To maintain data integrity, you must set up rules and systems that guard your data against unwanted changes. This involves controlling who can access or modify the data, protecting it during transfers, and keeping records of any changes made.

Actionable Steps for Maintaining Data Integrity

Implement Access Controls

Controlling who can see and change your data helps prevent unauthorised alterations.

1. **Set User Permissions**: Decide who can view, edit, or delete data. For example, only certain team members can change important files.
2. **Use Strong Passwords**: Make sure everyone uses passwords that are hard to guess to protect data from unauthorised access.

3. **Regularly Update Access Rights**: Check who has access to data and adjust permissions when people join or leave the team.

Maintain Regular Backups

Having copies of your data helps you recover it if something goes wrong.

1. **Schedule Frequent Backups**: Regularly save copies of important data and store them safely.
2. **Test Restoring Data**: Practice getting your data back from backups to make sure it works when needed.
3. **Store Backups Securely**: Keep backup copies safe, like a secure cloud service or an off-site location.

Monitor and Log Data Activities

Keeping track of who does what with your data helps detect unauthorised actions.

1. **Set Up Activity Logs**: Record when data is accessed or changed and by whom.
2. **Review Logs Regularly**: Look at these records to spot any unusual activities that shouldn't happen.
3. **Alert on Suspicious Behaviour**: Use tools that notify you if something unusual is detected like too many failed login attempts.

By following these steps, you can protect your data from unwanted changes and make sure it's trustworthy. Keeping your data safe helps everyone rely on it to make good decisions and keeps your company running smoothly. Remember, protecting data integrity is like guarding a treasure; it keeps your valuable information secure and dependable.

Continuous Improvement

Continuous improvement means always finding ways to make things better. It's about not settling for 'good enough' but aiming for 'even better.' In the world of data, new tools and ideas always come up. What worked well last year might not be the best choice now. By regularly checking how you handle data, you can find new ways to save time, reduce mistakes, and make smarter decisions.

Imagine if you never updated your computer or apps. They might run slowly or not work with new file types. Similarly, if you don't keep improving your data processes, you might miss out on helpful new features or ways to make your work easier. Just like keeping your toys in good shape makes playtime more fun, keeping your data processes updated makes your work smoother and more efficient.

Listening to your team is important because they work with the data every day. They might have great ideas about how to make things easier or spot problems that need fixing. Encouraging everyone to share their thoughts helps find new solutions. Trying new ideas can lead to big improvements. Even small changes can make a difference over time. By testing new methods on a small scale, you can see what works best before making bigger changes.

Remember, continuous improvement isn't about making huge changes all at once. It's like taking small steps forward. Over time, these small steps add up to big progress. And by celebrating these improvements, you motivate everyone to keep looking for ways to improve.

Actionable Steps for Continuous Improvement

Regularly Review Your Data Processes

It's important to check how you handle data to find areas where you can improve.

1. **Set Up Routine Check-Ups**: Plan specific times, such as every three or six months, to review your data practices. Mark these dates on a calendar to ensure they aren't forgotten.
2. **Create a Checklist**: Develop a list of items to examine, like data entry methods, storage solutions, and sharing protocols. This ensures a thorough review every time.
3. **Identify and Solve Problems**: Look for steps that are slow or prone to mistakes. Once identified, brainstorm and implement solutions to enhance efficiency and accuracy.

Encourage New Ideas and Innovation

Trying new things can lead to better ways of working.

1. **Allow Time for Experimenting**: Allocate specific times each week or month for team members to explore new tools or methods that could improve data management. This dedicated time fosters creativity and experimentation.
2. **Support Learning**: Provide resources such as online courses, books, or workshops to help your team build new skills. Encouraging continuous learning ensures your team stays updated on the latest advancements.
3. **Share and Celebrate Successes**: When someone discovers a better way to handle data, share their success with the entire team and recognise their effort. Celebrating these wins motivates others to seek improvements as well.

Implement Pilot Programs

Testing new ideas on a small scale helps see if they work.

1. **Choose a Small Area to Test**: Select a specific part of your data process, such as a single team or project, to implement a new tool or method. This focused approach minimises risk while allowing you to assess effectiveness.

2. **Monitor Results**: Carefully observe how the changes impact your work. Look for speed, accuracy, or user satisfaction improvements to determine the pilot program's success.
3. **Decide on Next Steps**: If the pilot is successful, plan how to roll out the changes to the entire team. If it doesn't work as expected, analyse what went wrong and consider alternative solutions.

By following these steps, you can keep improving how you handle data. Continuous improvement makes your work easier and helps your company succeed. Small, consistent changes lead to significant advancements over time, ensuring that your data management practices remain effective and up-to-date.

Summary

This chapter delved into the 'process' component of building a data-driven company, emphasising the importance of effective data governance and management. We explored three key principles: 1) Data Governance Principles, 2) Roles and Responsibilities, and 3) Data Quality and Management. Each principle ensures data is managed consistently, responsibly, and efficiently across the organisation.

Firstly, Data Governance Principles focus on standardising data practices, setting clear data policies, and ensuring compliance and ethics. Organisations reduce confusion and improve efficiency by establishing consistent methods for collecting, storing, and using data. Clear data policies act like rules everyone follows, helping to protect sensitive information and maintain trust. Ensuring compliance with laws and ethical standards safeguards the company from legal issues and builds a reputation of integrity.

Secondly, Roles and Responsibilities highlight the importance of knowing everyone's data-related duties. Implementing data stewardship assigns dedicated individuals to care for data quality and usability. Clearly defining roles prevents overlap and confusion, much like players on a sports team knowing their positions. Establishing accountability structures ensures that data governance tasks are monitored and team members are recognised for their contributions.

Lastly, Data Quality and Management are essential for making smart decisions based on reliable data. Ensuring data quality involves setting standards for accuracy, completeness, and consistency. Maintaining data integrity means protecting data from unauthorised changes and ensuring it remains trustworthy. Committing to continuous improvement encourages the organisation to regularly review and enhance data processes, staying up-to-date with new tools and ideas.

By focusing on these three principles, companies create a strong foundation for effective data governance. This leads to better decision-making, reduced risks, and a culture where data is trusted and leveraged for strategic success.

Chapter 7:
Leveraging Technology and Tools

In this chapter, we'll explore the last important component we discussed at the start of the book, 'tools and technologies'. These help us collect, store, and understand information better. By using them, we can make smarter decisions that help your business grow.

We have learned that data is like oil for a company. It helps you create new products, gain more customers, and stay ahead of others. But just having a lot of data isn't enough. We need the right tools to handle it properly, like software and hardware. These tools make sure we use data in every choice we make.

Defining Tools and Technology Component

To use data well, you need the tools and technologies to help you manage it. Let's understand what they are and why they matter:

1. **Understanding Data Tools and Technologies:** These software and hardware solutions help you handle data from start to finish. It can range from data storage solutions, such as databases, to visualisation tools that show you information in ways that more people can understand, like charts and graphs. Each tool has a specific purpose, from capturing data to making it useful.
2. **Facilitators of Business Processes:** Technology that allows you to streamline and automate your daily business activities with data, whether collecting or analysing it. Using these tools ensures that accurate information is always available to help you make decisions. This makes your work more efficient, reduces mistakes, and gives you up-to-date insights, which are crucial in a busy business world.
3. **Important Strategic Assets:** Advanced technologies, like artificial intelligence and machine learning, will provide you with a competitive edge by helping you learn and predict trends. They allow companies to innovate, guess what might happen next, and make services just right for each customer. Investing in these tools can lead to new opportunities and help the company stay ahead in the market.

The Role and Importance of Having the Right Tools & Technologies

Choosing the right tools and technologies makes it easier for your data strategy to succeed. Instead of working blindly, you can rely on these solutions to uncover what customers truly want. With that knowledge, you can create products or services that better fit their needs. By carefully picking tools that align with your company's goals, you ensure everyone's time and effort are spent wisely.

Using well-suited technologies also helps your company respond quickly when situations change. For example, real-time data tools allow you to make better decisions on the spot. This approach gives you an advantage in meeting new challenges, whether that means adjusting a marketing plan, improving a product, or entering a new market.

When all team members have access to the right tools, they feel more confident using data. Decisions become clearer because they're based on reliable information, making it easier to complete projects and reach business targets. Investing in tools that truly serve your needs builds a strong foundation for long-term success. Instead of chasing every new trend, focusing on what works best for your company keeps you moving in the right direction, ensuring your data strategy remains valuable and effective.

Common Challenges

This chapter will discuss some common problems businesses face with their tools and technologies. Just like in the last three chapters, understanding these challenges is the first step to finding and fixing them.

Difficulty Scaling Operations

As businesses expand, they often struggle to adjust their systems and processes to handle more data and customers. When existing tools aren't built to scale, they may become sluggish or fail outright, making it difficult to keep pace with growing demands. For example, a company that once served only a small group of clients may suddenly find its servers overloaded or its software unable to process larger amounts of information.

Beyond technical issues, slow or outdated operations can also create unnecessary delays. When it takes too long to gather and interpret important data, decision-makers cannot react swiftly to changes in the market or respond effectively to customer needs. Equally challenging is the inability to add resources when activity increases. Without the capacity to bring in more computing power, storage, or staff at the right time, a business cannot adjust smoothly to periods of heavy workload. It must turn away opportunities or risk quality slipping.

Inflexible Systems

When a company relies on tools and technologies that cannot adapt, it risks becoming trapped in methods that no longer support its evolving goals. As time passes and new opportunities appear, outdated solutions struggle to accommodate fresh ideas, much like trying to run a modern video game on an old console. Many years ago, I saw a company invest heavily in setting up a 2G private network. By the time they were done, 4G was already in the market. This made them lose out on all the new possibilities that are only possible with 4G or better.

Overdependence on a single vendor further complicates this issue, making it difficult to switch to more suitable options without incurring high costs or lengthy delays. Implementing updates also becomes a slow and difficult process. Instead of swiftly adopting improved tools, the business must wait, leaving behind competitors who move faster and more confidently. Without the ability to adjust its systems, a company may miss out on valuable innovations, struggle to keep pace and fail to meet new demands fully.

Integration Obstacles

Smooth collaboration between different parts of a business depends on systems that can share information effortlessly, yet this is often easier said than done. When data remains locked away in separate, unconnected software, no one can see the full picture. Important insights slip through the cracks, making spotting problems early or acting on emerging trends tough. Teams might use different processes that don't match up, causing confusion, mistakes, and delays. Imagine solving a puzzle with pieces scattered across rooms and no clear way to bring them together.

Integrating multiple systems can be complicated, time-consuming, and expensive. Companies may pour resources into custom solutions that still do not function seamlessly, forcing them to rely on workarounds rather than true cooperation. Without proper integration, decision-makers struggle to respond quickly and effectively, leaving valuable opportunities on the table and hindering a company's ability to work as a unified whole.

Infrastructure Uncertainties

Deciding how to set up and manage the technical backbone of a business can be challenging when there are so many possibilities. Some companies hesitate between building their own in-house systems or relying on external cloud services, unsure which will best support their growth. This uncertainty can slow progress as managers debate cost, security, and reliability, always determining if they have made the right call.

When existing systems underperform, everyday tasks take longer, frustrating both employees and customers. Balancing budgets becomes difficult, too, as businesses try to avoid overspending on technology that might not deliver the needed results. Ultimately, these doubts can prevent a company from adopting better, more efficient solutions. By carefully evaluating their options and seeking guidance when necessary, businesses can reduce confusion, invest in technology that genuinely helps, and build an infrastructure that handles current needs and can grow gracefully in the future.

Limited Access to Insights

Even when a company collects huge amounts of data, its true value remains untapped if employees cannot easily access or understand it properly. Complicated tools or messy interfaces can turn useful information into a confusing jumble, much like a locked library filled with helpful books no one can read. If your team cannot retrieve what they need at the right time, valuable chances to improve products, customer experiences, or internal processes slip by unnoticed. Slow or limited access to critical information makes it impossible to respond quickly when situations change. A lack of proper training only adds to the problem, leaving employees needing help navigating the systems or interpreting data accurately.

Over time, all these issues undercut confidence in decision-making. Instead of using data to guide their strategies, teams rely on guesswork. To truly benefit from the power of data, a company must ensure everyone can find, understand, and apply the insights they need.

By understanding these common challenges, businesses can work on solutions to overcome them. This helps build a stronger foundation for growth and success, making sure that tools and technologies truly help the company move forward.

Principle 1: Designing a Flexible Data Approach

In a world that changes quickly, your business needs data systems that can grow and adapt. Designing a flexible data approach means building systems that can handle more work and adjust to new needs as your business expands. This helps you avoid costly overhauls and keeps everything running smoothly, no matter what the future brings.

Ensuring Scalability

Nowadays, businesses need data plans that can grow and change with them. Think of it like building with blocks; you want to add more blocks or move them around as you need to. A flexible data approach helps your business keep up without constantly starting over. This principle is about ensuring your data systems can grow as you do, so let's look at how to ensure scalability.

Ensuring scalability means designing your data systems to handle more work as your business grows. Imagine planting a small tree and knowing it will become big one day. You wouldn't put it in a tiny pot because it wouldn't have room to grow. In the same way, you need to think ahead about your data needs. By planning for growth, choosing the right tools, and using your resources wisely, you can make sure your data systems won't hold you back further down the line.

Actionable Steps for Building Scalable Data Systems

Forecast Future Needs

It's important to consider what you'll need in the future, not just right now. By looking ahead, you can get ready and avoid problems later. This helps you build systems that won't become too small too quickly.

1. **Business Growth Projections:** Look at how your business has grown and what might happen next. For example, if your online store doubled its customers last year, it might double again. Plan for more data and more users so your systems can handle them.
2. **Market Trends Analysis:** Pay attention to what's happening in your industry. If more people are shopping online, you might get more customers. Knowing the trends helps you prepare your data systems for changes.
3. **Resource Planning:** Set aside money and time to expand your data systems later. This could mean spending less now and more

in the future when the storage requirement goes up or when you need to hire more data experts when you need them.

Invest in Scalable Solutions

Choosing the right tools now can make things easier as you grow. Scalable solutions are like stretchy pants; they fit now and can stretch to fit later.

1. **Flexible Technologies:** Pick tools that can grow with you. Services like Amazon Web Services or Microsoft Azure let you add more space and power when needed, so you don't run out.
2. **Modular Systems:** Use systems made of parts you can add to or change easily. This way, you can improve one part without changing everything else.
3. **Find Consultants & Experts:** Talk to people who know a lot about data systems. Based on your requirements, they can help you choose the most appropriate tools and plan for the future to avoid costly mistakes.

Monitor Performance Regularly

Keeping an eye on how your systems work helps you spot problems early. It's like checking your car's engine before a long trip.

1. **Use Monitoring Tools:** Tools like Datadog or New Relic can watch how your data systems are doing. They can tell you if something is slowing down or not working right.
2. **Set Performance Benchmarks:** Decide what good performance looks like for your systems. With it, you can see if they meet your goals or need improvements.
3. **Adjust as Needed:** If you see problems or your business grows faster than you thought, be ready to make changes. This could mean upgrading parts of your system or changing how things are set up.

Optimise Resource Usage

Making the best use of what you have helps your systems run smoothly without wasting money. It's like making sure all the lights are off when you leave a room to save electricity.

1. **Implement Efficient Processes:** Use methods that improve your data systems, like data compression to save space or efficient coding to run faster.
2. **Scale Resources Dynamically:** Use tools that automatically give you more power or space when you need it and less when you don't. This way, you only pay for what you use.
3. **Review Costs Regularly:** Keep an eye on how much you're spending on your data systems. Look for ways to save money without hurting performance.

By following these steps, you can make sure your data systems are ready to grow with your business. Planning ahead, choosing the right tools, and keeping an eye on things helps you avoid big problems later. Just like adding more blocks to a strong building, your business can grow smoothly and successfully when your data systems are scalable.

Case Study: Amex GBT's Scalable Data Solution

American Express Global Business Travel (Amex GBT) operates in over 120 countries. They needed their data systems to grow with their business. One big challenge was creating a single portal from 945 different data files, which would take over six months with their old tools. Moving to the cloud was also hard because their current system couldn't handle the performance needed. Plus, keeping user data safe was very important. It's just not scalable.

To solve these problems, Amex GBT invested in a smart analytics tool called Premier Insights. This tool helped them manage their travel programs better by showing key cost, time, and value information. It made it easier for users to see how their travel plans were performing.

The results were impressive. Travel expenses were reduced by 30%, and new users could start using the platform in just one day instead of a week. The easy-to-use dashboards and real-time reports led to more people worldwide using Premier Insights. Amex GBT's scalable data solution helped them save money and grow smoothly.

Promoting Flexibility

Making your data systems flexible is like having a tool that can do many jobs. Just like a Swiss Army knife can help in different situations, your data systems should be able to change and adjust when new things happen. This allows your business to handle new chances and challenges without starting all over.

Having processes that can change easily is important. If your data methods are adaptable, you can adjust them when the market changes. For example, using ways of working that let you change plans quickly helps your team meet new business needs.

It's also good not to rely too much on one thing. You keep your options open by not depending on just one vendor or tool. This means you can switch to new tools without too much trouble.

Being open to new ideas and tools helps your business stay ahead. New technologies come out all the time, and some might help you do things better. If you're willing to try new things, you can find better ways to work and solve problems.

Actionable Steps for Flexible Data Systems

Choose Versatile Tools

Picking the right tools is very important to keep your data systems flexible. By choosing tools that can do many things and work well with others, you can adjust to changes more easily.

1. **Broad Compatibility:** Select technologies that can connect with many other systems and tools. For example, choose data software that works with different databases and programs so you can use it in many different situations.
2. **Customisable Options:** Look for tools you can change to fit your needs. Some programs let you add features or change settings so they work just how you want them to.
3. **Use Open Standards:** Choose tools that follow common rules many people use. This makes it easier to connect with other systems and replace parts if needed without getting stuck with one vendor.
4. **Multi-Platform Support:** Pick tools that work on different devices and operating systems. This way, your data systems can run on various computers and tablets without problems.
5. **Scalability:** Ensure the tools can grow with your needs. If your data gets bigger, the tool should handle more information without trouble.

Avoid Vendor Lock-In

Not depending too much on one supplier keeps your options open for the future. This way, you can switch to better solutions if they come along.

1. **Diversify Vendors:** Use products and services from different companies. For example, don't get all your software from one place.
2. **Use Open-Source Tools:** Use free tools that have lower switching costs. This gives you more control and flexibility over your data systems.
3. **Negotiate Flexible Contracts:** When making deals with vendors, include terms that let you change or add other vendors if needed.
4. **Integrate with Multiple Systems:** Design your systems to work with various other systems. This reduces reliance on any single provider - more on this in the next section.

Embrace Innovation

Being open to new technologies helps your business stay ahead and find better ways to work. Trying new things can lead to big improvements.

1. **Explore New Technologies:** Keep an eye on new tools and methods that might help your business. This could include new software or ways of processing data.
2. **Allocate Time for Experimentation:** Allow your team time to try new ideas or technologies, such as setting aside a few hours each week to explore new tools.
3. **Invest in Research and Development:** Spend resources on developing new methods or tools to give your business an edge.

Following these detailed steps, you can make your data systems more flexible and ready for anything. This means your business can adjust to new opportunities and challenges without big problems, staying strong and successful in a changing world.

Enhancing Integration

It's important to make sure all parts of your data systems work well together. It's like building a train system where all the tracks connect, and the trains run smoothly between stations. When your data flows easily between different parts of your business, everyone can do their jobs better, and your company becomes stronger.

Having a unified view of data means that everyone sees the same information. It's like having one big map that shows all the train lines and stations, so nobody gets lost. This helps teams connect and collaborate more effectively with one another, removing silos and barriers. This also allows teams to make good decisions because they all have the right facts.

Streamlined processes make it easy for data to move from one place to another. It's like making sure trains are always on time, and stops are quick so people get where they need to go without delays. This might involve setting up systems that automatically move data where required.

Consistency is about doing things the same way each time. Like having the same signs and rules at every train station, it helps people know what to expect. When everyone handles data in the same way, it's less confusing, and mistakes happen less often.

Actionable Steps for Connecting Systems Together

Implement Integration Strategies

Next, make changes to help your systems work better together.

1. **Standardise Practices:** Create rules for how everyone should handle data. For example, decide on the same format for entering dates or customer names.
2. **Use Integration Tools:** Find tools that help connect different systems. Some programs automatically send data from one system to another so everyone has the latest information.
3. **Set Up a Central Data Place:** Create one main spot where all important data is stored. This could be a big database that everyone can access when needed.

Use Automation Where Possible

Setting up data pipelines and automating tasks can make data integration smoother and save time.

1. **Automate Data Transfers:** Set up systems that simultaneously automatically move data between platforms.
2. **Use Automated Alerts:** Create alerts that let you know if something goes wrong, like if data isn't updating correctly.

3. **Leverage Workflow Tools:** Use software to streamline and automate repetitive tasks so your team can focus on more important work.

Case Study: HomeGoods Plus's Automated Data Pipeline

HomeGoods Plus, a mid-sized retail company, wanted to make smarter decisions and stay ahead in the market. They set up an automated data pipeline to move and manage their data smoothly. First, they used a data integration platform to gather real-time information from sales, marketing, and inventory systems. Then, they implemented workflow tools to handle repetitive tasks automatically and set up alerts to spot any problems quickly.

By automating their data processes, HomeGoods Plus reduced the time it took to get insights from days to minutes. This allowed them to make faster, data-driven decisions. Their marketing campaigns became 15% more effective, and sales increased by 10% in the first three months. The automated system also made their data more reliable and helped them quickly adapt to new trends and customer needs. HomeGoods Plus's use of automation boosted their efficiency and growth.

Principle 2: Making Informed Infrastructure Decisions

Choosing the right infrastructure and tools to handle your company's data is important. It'll impact how well your data initiatives align with your business goals, support growth, and meet regulatory requirements.

Evaluating Cloud vs. On-Premises

A key decision in your data strategy is choosing between cloud-based and on-premises infrastructure. Each option offers unique benefits and challenges; the best choice depends on your organisation's needs.

Cloud infrastructure provides flexibility and scalability. It allows you to quickly adjust resources based on your current requirements without significant upfront investment in hardware. This flexibility can be especially beneficial for organisations experiencing rapid growth or fluctuating workloads. Cloud providers often offer advanced security features and take care of maintenance and updates, reducing the burden on your internal IT team.

On the other hand, on-premises infrastructure gives you greater control over your data and systems. This control is crucial for organisations with strict regulatory obligations or those who handle highly sensitive data. Managing your own infrastructure allows for customisation to meet specific performance needs and can provide cost advantages for stable, predictable workloads over time.

When deciding between cloud and on-premises solutions, consider the following key factors:

1. **Cost:** Analyse both the initial and long-term costs associated with each option. Depending on usage patterns, cloud solutions typically have lower initial costs but may lead to higher expenses over time. On-premises solutions require substantial upfront investment but can be more cost-effective in the long run for certain workloads.
2. **Scalability:** Consider how quickly you may need to scale your operations. Cloud solutions offer rapid scalability, enabling you to increase or decrease resources. Scaling on-premises infrastructure can take time and may involve additional investment in hardware and resources.

3. **Security:** Evaluate the sensitivity of your data and your security requirements. While cloud providers invest heavily in security measures, you may prefer on-premises solutions if you need direct control over all aspects of data security.
4. **Compliance:** Understand any regulatory requirements that affect your data management. Some industries have strict rules about where data must be stored and how it is handled, which can influence your choice between cloud and on-premises solutions.

By carefully assessing these considerations, you can make a well-informed decision that aligns with your organisation's goals and ensures that your data infrastructure supports your current and future needs.

Actionable Steps for Choosing the Right Infrastructure

Analyse Your Business Requirements

First, think carefully about what your company requires so you can select the best option.

1. **Check How Secret Your Data Is:** Find out if the information you handle is very private or important. If it is, you might need extra protection to keep it safe, like a strong lock on a treasure chest.
2. **Look at Your Money Plans:** Figure out how much you can spend now and later. Some choices might be cheaper at first but more over time, like a toy that often needs new batteries.
3. **Think About Growing Bigger:** If your company will get bigger soon, you need tools that can grow with you, like adjustable shoes that fit even as your feet grow.

Consult Stakeholders

Next, ask people who know a lot about these things to help you make a good decision.

1. **Ask Your IT and Security Teams:** These people know about computers and keeping things safe. They can tell you which options are secure and work well.
2. **Check with Legal and Compliance Teams:** They know the rules and laws your company must follow. They can tell you if there are special rules about where or how you keep your data.
3. **Include Managers and Workers:** Talk to the people who use the tools every day. They can share what they need to do their jobs better.

Make an Informed Decision

Finally, use the information you have gathered to pick the best tools for your company.

1. **Compare the Good and Bad:** List the pros and cons for each option. This will help you see which one fits your needs the best. Use a decision matrix to evaluate your options.
2. **Plan How to Start Using It:** Once you've decided, make a step-by-step plan to set it up. Decide who will do what and when it will happen.
3. **Be Ready to Adjust:** Sometimes things change, or unexpected problems come up. Be prepared to change your plan, like changing the route if a road is closed.

Following these steps, you can choose the right tools to help your company now and as it grows. Remember, picking the right infrastructure is important to reaching your goals.

Case Study: Capital One's Move to AWS Cloud

Capital One, a major US bank, moved all its data from its own centres to the AWS cloud by 2020. This was the first time a large bank had fully switched to the cloud. They started this journey in 2012 and used over 30 AWS services like Amazon EC2 and Amazon S3. They also trained their tech team and changed how they developed software to be faster and more flexible.

The move to AWS brought many benefits. They improved disaster recovery by 70%, cut transaction errors and problem-solving time by half, and sped up building environments from three months to minutes. Innovation sped up too, with new code released multiple times a day. Capital One also created new customer tools like Eno, an intelligent assistant, and better mobile apps. This switch helped them work smoothly during the COVID-19 pandemic and keep customers happy.

Considering Hybrid Solutions

In the last part, we discussed choosing between cloud and on-premises systems. Sometimes, combining cloud and on-premises systems is the best way to go. This is called a hybrid solution. It's like having both a bicycle and a car. You use each one when it makes the most sense.

With a hybrid approach, you get the flexibility of the cloud and the control of on-premises systems. You can keep important and sensitive information on your own servers, like keeping special treasures safe at home. At the same time, you can use the cloud for things that need to change quickly or when you need extra space, like renting a bigger room for a party.

By using both, you reduce risks. If one system has a problem, the other can keep things running. It's like having two ways to get to school; if your bike has a flat tyre, you can still walk and not be late. This way, your company can keep working smoothly even if something unexpected happens.

Using a hybrid solution can also save money. You use cheaper, on-premises systems for more stable and predictable reporting demands. You only spend time on the cloud when you need extra help, like when doing machine learning or exploration-type projects. This helps you use your resources wisely and not pay too much.

Actionable Steps for Using Hybrid Solution

Decide Which Tasks Go Where

To make the most of a hybrid solution, you must determine which jobs are best to keep on your own servers and which should go to the cloud. This helps you use each system where it works best.

1. **Keep Important Data Safe at Home:** Store sensitive information, like customer details or secret plans, on your own servers. This gives you full control over who can access it and how it's protected.
2. **Use the Cloud for Flexible Work:** Put tasks that need lots of computing power or change often, like running big reports or hosting websites, in the cloud. The cloud can easily handle growing workloads without needing to buy more hardware.
3. **Balance Your Workload:** Look at all your tasks and decide the best place for each one. This way, everything runs smoothly, and you benefit from both systems.

Make Sure Systems Work Together

It's important that your cloud services and on-premises systems can talk to each other. Data can move between them easily, and your team can use both without trouble.

1. **Plan How They Connect:** Set up secure connections, like VPNs (Virtual Private Networks), so your systems can share information safely. Think of it like building a bridge between two islands.
2. **Use the Same Rules Everywhere:** Apply the same security measures and policies in both systems. For example, everyone should use strong passwords and follow the same sign-in steps while accessing the cloud or on-premises systems.

3. **Find Helpful Tools:** Use management tools that work with both systems, like special software that helps you see what's happening in the cloud and on-premises at the same time.

Plan Ahead for the Future

Think about how your company might change and grow. Planning ahead ensures your hybrid solution will continue to meet your needs.

1. **Set Clear Goals:** Decide what you want your hybrid system to achieve, like handling more customers or supporting new services. Write down these goals so everyone knows them.
2. **Stay Flexible:** Be ready to adopt new technologies or make changes as needed. For example, if a better cloud service comes along, consider if it's worth switching.
3. **Budget for Growth:** Allocate money for future upgrades or expansions. This way, you won't be caught off guard when you need to invest in your systems.

Watch and Manage Costs Wisely

By monitoring expenses, you can ensure you get the best value from your hybrid solution without overspending.

1. **Track Spending:** Regularly review how much you pay for cloud services and maintaining your on-premises systems. Look at bills and reports to see where your money is going.
2. **Adjust Resources as Needed:** If you're not fully utilising specific cloud services, consider lowering the threshold or switching them off completely to save money. Conversely, ensure essential services have enough resources to perform well.
3. **Plan for Cost Savings:** Consider options that might cost more now but save money later, like pre-paying for cloud services at a discount or investing in energy-efficient hardware.

By following these actionable steps, you'll make your hybrid solution work effectively for your company. You'll enjoy the flexibility of the cloud and the control of on-premises systems and be prepared for the future. Remember, combining both systems can give you the best of both worlds, helping your company stay strong and competitive.

Ensuring Performance and Reliability

After setting up the right mix of cloud and on-premises systems, it's important to make sure everything works well all the time. Keeping your systems running smoothly helps your business stay strong and your team to do their best work.

One way to do this is by minimising downtime. Downtime happens when systems stop working, like when the power goes out at home and you can't turn on the lights. When your systems are always up and running, your team can keep working without interruptions, and your customers stay happy because they can use your services whenever needed.

Being prepared for surprises is also very important. Sometimes, unexpected things happen, like a storm on a sunny day. If you have a plan for these surprises, you can handle them without too much trouble. This might mean having backup systems ready to go or knowing what steps to take when something goes wrong. Being prepared helps your company bounce back quickly from any problems.

Lastly, always look for ways to make your systems better. Just like practising the piano helps you play more beautiful music, improving your systems makes them work faster and more efficiently. This could involve updating your software, adding new features, or finding better ways to do things. By constantly improving, your company stays ahead and can handle whatever comes next.

By focusing on keeping your systems reliable and always working to improve them, you help your business stay strong and successful. It's like building a solid house that can withstand any weather. The stronger your systems are, the better your company can serve its customers and reach its goals.

Actionable Steps for Ensuring Performance and Reliability

Invest in Good, Reliable Technologies

Choosing strong and dependable tools ensures your systems run smoothly. This reduces problems and helps everything work better.

1. **Choose Trusted Providers:** Select software and equipment from companies known for high quality. Research their reputation by reading reviews and asking others who use their products.
2. **Get Support Agreements:** Arrange for help if something goes wrong. This means having a contract where providers promise to fix problems quickly, like a warranty on a new bike.
3. **Keep Everything Updated:** Regularly install updates for your software and hardware. Updates often fix bugs and improve how things work, just like tuning a piano to keep it sounding nice.

Develop Contingency Plans

Having backup plans ready helps you respond quickly when issues occur. Being prepared minimises downtime and keeps things running.

1. **Make Regular Copies of Important Data:** Schedule daily or weekly backups of your essential information. Use safe places like external drives or cloud storage to keep these copies, similar to saving a spare key in case you lose the original.
2. **Write Down Clear Recovery Steps:** Create easy-to-follow instructions on what to do if systems fail. Include who to contact and the exact steps to fix problems, like a map showing the way if you get lost.

3. **Practice Your Plans:** Hold drills where your team pretends there's a problem and follows the recovery steps. This helps everyone know what to do in a real situation and shows where to improve.

Monitor Systems Regularly

Watching your systems helps you spot small issues before they become big problems. Regular monitoring keeps things running smoothly.

1. **Use Special Monitoring Software:** Use monitoring software that keeps an eye on your systems and alerts you if something isn't right, like a smoke detector that beeps if there's a fire.
2. **Set Up Alerts for Important Events:** Configure the system to send messages if certain things happen, such as a server getting too hot or running out of space. This lets you act quickly to fix issues.
3. **Review Reports and Logs Often:** Regularly check system reports to see how everything works. Look for patterns that might show a problem is starting, like noticing if a plant's leaves are wilting before it dies.

By following these steps, you can ensure your company's systems are reliable and perform well. This helps everyone do their jobs without interruptions and keeps your business moving forward.

Principle 3: Empowering Teams with Self-Service Analytics

Imagine if your team could find answers to their questions without waiting for someone in the data team. Giving them the tools to look at data independently is like giving them a map to find hidden treasure. They can make smarter choices faster, moving your company quicker and further. Have you ever wanted to solve a problem immediately instead of waiting for help? By empowering more of your team with self-service analytics, you're letting more people within your company take the lead.

Implementing Self-Service Tools

It's important to give your team intuitive and easy-to-use tools. The easier it is to use the tool, the more people will use it. More importantly, having tools like dashboards will help your team get all the data they need to make decisions and do their job better. They'll be less reliant on central data teams. Essentially, it's like being able to solve your own problem without having to wait in line. This helps things move faster and makes your company more effective.

Actionable Steps for Self-Service Dashboards

Identify Business Intelligence (BI) Needs

Before picking the tools, knowing what your team needs is important. Understanding their questions helps in finding the best solutions.

1. **Consult with Departments:** Talk to different teams to learn what data they need. For example, the sales team might want to see how many products are sold each day.
2. **Assess Current Limitations:** Look at your current tools and see where they might not be helping enough. Are there times when teams can't get answers quickly?
3. **Set Priorities Based on Importance:** Decide which needs are the most important to help the team immediately. Focus on areas where data access will make the biggest difference.

Balance Development and License Costs with User Needs

It's important to find the right balance between how much the tools cost and how much they help your team. You don't want to spend too much money on tools that are too hard or not helpful.

1. **Evaluate Tool Costs:** Look at how much different tools cost, including licenses and any extra expenses. Consider whether paying more gives you better features that your team really needs.
2. **Consider Development Effort:** Consider how much work it will take to set up and keep the tools running. Choose tools that are easy to manage so your IT team is manageable.
3. **Match Tools to User Skills:** Pick tools that fit your team's needs. If most users are beginners, choose simpler tools. This way, you ensure the tools are useful and worth the cost.

Select Appropriate Self-Service BI Tools

Choosing the right tools means finding ones that are easy to use and fit well with your other systems. This makes sure everyone can use them without problems.

1. **User-Friendly Interfaces:** Pick tools that are simple and easy to understand. Tools with clear buttons and simple instructions help people use them right away.
2. **Customisable Dashboards:** Find tools that let people set up their screens in the way they like. This helps them see the most important information quickly.
3. **Integration Capabilities:** Make sure the tools can connect easily to the data you already have. This way, all the information is in one place.

Pilot and Rollout

Testing the tools with a small group first helps catch any problems. Then, you can share the tools with everyone once they work well.

1. **Trial Periods with Select Users:** Create a focus group to try to build the dashboard first. See how it works before slowly releasing it to a wider audience.

2. **Gather Feedback and Make Adjustments:** Collect feedback from the focus group to understand what they like and don't like - iterate based on feedback to build a more effective solution.
3. **Gradual Implementation:** Share the tools with one team at a time. This helps everyone get used to the new tools without feeling rushed.

By giving your team easy-to-use tools and training, you help them find answers independently. This makes your company faster and stronger because everyone can make smart choices without waiting. When your team feels empowered, they can do their best work and your whole company benefits.

Case Study: AT&T's Self-Service Analytics Transformation

AT&T wanted to make data easy for everyone to use. They set up a self-service analytics platform using Snowflake's Telecom Data Cloud. First, AT&T moved their reporting tool to Snowflake and combined data from call centres, stores, and other sources. They created a library with over 2,700 metrics and built over 230 APIs for easy access to data. They also made 80 custom screens for real-time sales reports and customer surveys.

With these self-service tools, about 115,000 employees can access data quickly. Most user queries are answered in less than one second, and the platform saved AT&T 84% on estimated annual costs thanks to results caching. Users make over a million API calls each day, helping AT&T make faster and smarter decisions. This transformation improved customer service and helped AT&T stay ahead in the telecom industry by making data accessible and affordable for everyone.

Enhancing Data Accessibility

Imagine a big library where everyone can find the books they need, but only those they're allowed to read. Making data easy to access in your company is just like that library. It's important to help your team get the information they need for their jobs while keeping important secrets safe. When your team can easily find and use the data they need, they can make better decisions faster.

Letting people see the data they need and keeping other information private is very important. It's like giving each person a special key that only opens the doors they should enter. This way, known as role-based access control (RBAC), ensures everyone can do their work well and, at the same time, protect important information. When team members have the right access, they don't have to wait or ask for data, so they can do their jobs more quickly.

Having all your data in a central data repository is like having all the books in one big library instead of many little ones scattered around. This makes it easier for your team to find what they need and ensure everyone uses the same correct information. It also helps prevent mistakes when people use old or different data versions.

Like you lock up valuable things, you must keep your data safe. This means having security measures to make sure only the right people can see it. Protecting your data keeps your company safe and helps your customers trust you. When everyone knows the data is secure, they can focus on their work without worrying about safety.

Actionable Steps for Robust Data Access

Define Who Can See What Data

It's important to decide which team members need access to certain data based on their jobs. This helps keep sensitive information safe while making sure everyone has what they need.

1. **Understand Each Role:** Look at what each person does in the company. For example, the sales team might need customer contact information, but they don't need to see employee salaries. Knowing this helps you give the right access to the right people.
2. **Set Clear Rules:** Make simple rules that explain who can see what data. Write these rules down so everyone knows and follows them. Clear rules prevent confusion and mistakes.
3. **Teach Your Team:** Explain these rules to your employees so they understand why they are important. When everyone knows the rules, they can help keep the data safe.

Put All the Data in One Place

Keeping all the data together helps your team find what they need quickly and easily.

1. **Create Central Storage:** Use one main place, like a big data warehouse, to store all important information. This way, people know exactly where to look for data.
2. **Organise the Data Well:** Arrange the data in folders with clear names so it's easy to find. Like books in a library are sorted by topic, your data should be neatly organised.
3. **Keep Data Updated:** Regularly check that the data is correct and up to date. This helps your team trust the information they use and prevents mistakes.

Protecting the Data with Strong Security Measures

Keeping data safe is just as important as making it accessible. We need to guard it against people who shouldn't see it.

1. **Use Strong Passwords and Security Tools**: Require passwords that are hard to guess and change them often. Use security programs that protect against viruses and hackers. This makes it harder for bad people to get in.

2. **Watch for Unusual Activity:** Monitor who is accessing the data. If someone tries to see the data they shouldn't, you can catch it early and stop them.
3. **Educate Your Team:** Teach your employees about data safety, like not sharing passwords or clicking on strange emails. When everyone knows how to be safe, the whole company is better protected.

By taking these steps, you help your team get the data they need while keeping it safe and organised. This makes work easier for everyone and helps your company do a better job. Remember, when data is easy to find and secure, your team can make smarter decisions faster.

Providing Support for Self-Service BI Tools

When you were young, did you ever have a new toy but didn't know how to play it? Did you feel frustrated or get bored with it after a few minutes? When your team gets new data tools, they might feel the same way if they don't have help. By offering good support, you ensure they can use these tools well and feel confident. This helps them find answers independently and make better decisions, which helps your company do better.

Helping your team quickly when they have questions is very important. They might stop using the new tools if they get stuck and no one can help. By being there when they need you, you keep them excited about using data. Also, they can use them even better by teaching them all the cool things the tools can do. When your team fully knows how to use the tools, they can find deeper insights and help your company grow. Encouraging everyone to use the new tools and making them feel supported helps them embrace new ways of working.

Actionable Steps for Supporting Self-Service BI Tools

To make sure your team gets the most out of the new tools, it's important to give them the help they need. Here are some steps you can take to support your team and help them feel confident and capable.

Set Up a Helpful Support Team

It's important to have people ready to assist when your team has questions or problems. This support can make using new tools easier and more enjoyable.

1. **Create a Special Help Desk:** Have a dedicated team or person who knows all about the BI tools. They should be easy to reach by phone, email, or in person. This way, when someone has a question, they know exactly who to ask and can get answers quickly. Too often, I've worked with clients where their IT and support teams are severely lagging. I had been personally bounced around by six teams just to get access to a specific platform.
2. **Make Sure Experts Are Available:** Have knowledgeable people who can help with tough questions. These experts can solve problems that others might need help to fix. Knowing that experts are there to help makes your team feel more secure.
3. **Offer Different Ways to Get Help:** Provide assistance through phone calls, emails, chats, or even face-to-face meetings. This gives your team options to choose how they want to get support, making it more convenient for them.

Create Easy-to-Understand Learning Materials

Helping your team learn how to use the tools on their own can make them feel more confident and independent.

1. **Make Simple Guides and Videos:** Create step-by-step instructions and short videos that show how to use the tools.

Using pictures and simple words makes it easier for everyone to follow along and learn at their own pace.
2. **Write Common Questions:** Put together a list of questions people often ask and the answers. This can help your team solve problems quickly without waiting for help, saving time and reducing frustration.
3. **Update Materials Regularly:** Keep the learning materials current by adding new tips and information. As the tools change or new features are added, updating the guides helps everyone stay up-to-date.

By providing strong support, you help your team feel confident using self-service BI tools. This means they can find the answers, make smarter decisions, and help your company succeed.

Summary

Overall, we explored the crucial role of tools and technologies in building a data-driven company. We delved into three key principles: 1) Designing a Flexible Data Approach, 2) Making Informed Infrastructure Decisions, and 3) Empowering Teams with Self-Service Analytics. Each principle is essential for effectively managing data, supporting business growth, and fostering a culture of informed decision-making.

Firstly, designing a flexible data approach emphasises the importance of creating data systems that can grow and adapt to the business. By ensuring scalability, companies can prepare their data infrastructure to handle increasing amounts of information without constant overhauls. Promoting flexibility allows organisations to adjust to new technologies and market changes, avoiding reliance on a single vendor or outdated systems. Enhancing integration ensures that different systems and tools work smoothly together, providing a unified view of data that helps teams collaborate and make better decisions.

Secondly, making informed infrastructure Decisions focuses on selecting the right mix of technologies to meet the organisation's needs. By evaluating cloud versus on-premises options, companies consider cost, scalability, security, and compliance factors to choose the best solution. Considering hybrid solutions enables businesses to combine the benefits of both cloud and on-premises systems, using each where it fits best. Ensuring performance and reliability involves investing in dependable technologies, developing contingency plans, and regularly monitoring systems to minimise downtime and keep operations running smoothly.

Lastly, empowering teams with self-service analytics highlights the importance of giving employees the tools and access they need to work with data independently. Implementing self-service tools provides user-friendly platforms that allow team members to find insights without always relying on IT support. Enhancing data accessibility ensures employees have appropriate access to the data they need while keeping sensitive information secure. Supporting self-service BI tools helps employees fully utilise these resources, offering assistance and training to maximise their effectiveness and encourage widespread adoption.

By focusing on these three principles, companies equip themselves with the right tools and technologies to effectively harness their data's power. This leads to smarter decision-making, quicker responses to market changes, and a culture where data is at the heart of strategic planning. Investing in scalable, flexible, and user-friendly technologies empowers teams to perform at their best, positioning the organisation for continued growth and success in a data-driven world.

Thank you so much for making it this far!

I really appreciate the time you took to read my book. As a small, individual publisher, it means a lot and I hope to make a positive impact for you and your company.

If you have 60 seconds, it'll mean the world to me if you share your honest feedback on Amazon. It does wonders for the book, and I love hearing your thoughts and experience with it!

To leave your feedback:

1) Open your camera app.
2) Point your mobile device at the QR code below.
3) This will open a review page in your browser app.

OR

Visit Link: wissenlau.com/sdp-feedback

THANK YOU!

Part 3:
Executing and Sustaining Your Data Strategy

Chapter 8:
Developing and Implementing Your Data Strategy

In earlier chapters, we identified several data initiatives by understanding the business's needs, assessing our readiness to work with data, pinpointing initiatives that encourage valuing data, shaping effective methods, and establishing the necessary tools.

Now, it's time to turn these ideas into real steps to help your company thrive. A detailed roadmap is essential for guiding this transition, outlining the specific actions, timelines, and resources required to implement each initiative effectively. This roadmap is a clear path for teams to follow, ensuring everyone works toward the same goals.

We're now in the final stage of the data strategy framework, executing and sustaining your data strategy. By putting our plans into action, we ensure that our data strategy becomes more than just a good idea on paper. This phase involves integrating our data efforts seamlessly into regular business activities, such as budget planning and setting future objectives, which helps our data strategy feel natural and connected rather than separate. Building on the groundwork we laid, we translate these foundations into actions that enhance how we use data. Careful planning allows us to establish a resilient system that adapts as the company evolves, supporting long-term growth and the ability to adjust to changing business environments.

With the right care and effort, our strategy will begin to show real benefits, guiding better decisions and helping the company grow well into the future. When these efforts are embedded into everyday work, the entire company benefits from stronger data insights, better results, and a solid foundation for long-term success.

Prioritising Your Data Initiative

So far, we've listed several actionable steps that you can take. However, to truly embed your data strategy within your organisation and maximise your resources, you must carefully prioritise these steps. Here, we'll explore some common frameworks that'll help you assess and rank each initiative, allowing you to focus on what truly matters.

Prioritising With the Data Maturity Model

Before diving into specific initiatives, use Chapter 3's data maturity assessment results to determine the components to focus on: mindset, people, process, or tools and technologies. The components at the lowest maturity stage represent the 'gaps' in your business. You should prioritise initiatives related to these components to yield the most significant improvements.

By focusing on the weakest link, you ensure that you're building a strong foundation for your data strategy. As mentioned earlier, a data strategy can only succeed when all four components are addressed. By addressing the area with the lowest maturity, you'll create a balanced development, ensuring resources are allocated to areas where they can have the greatest impact and allowing other components to function more effectively.

This will set your organisation up for the largest and most sustainable success.

Assessing Impact vs Effort

After deciding what component to prioritise, prioritise initiatives by evaluating each initiative by its potential impact on your organisation and the effort required to implement it.

1. **High Impact, Low Effort:** Focus on these initiatives first. They offer substantial value with minimal investment. For example, surveys can be created to assess employees' data literacy and gather their thoughts on introducing new data processes swiftly and with little effort. This feedback will reveal critical insights that drive more informed decision-making and shape your next strategic move.
2. **High Impact, High Effort:** These are essential for long-term success but may demand more resources and planning. For example, developing a comprehensive data literacy curriculum elevates the entire organisation's competency but requires substantial effort.
3. **Low Impact, Low Effort:** Consider these actions if resources allow, but they shouldn't distract from higher-priority tasks. For example, making minor tweaks to existing documentation won't have any major impact; it'll only make slight improvements at most.

4. **Low Impact, High Effort:** De-prioritise these initiatives. They consume resources without delivering significant benefits. For example, investing in technologies that don't integrate well with existing systems will have a low return.

By applying this framework across the four components, you can strategically prioritise initiatives that will effectively build the capabilities your organisation needs.

Aligning with Organisational Goals

After assessing impact and effort, focus on initiatives that directly support your organisation's strategic objectives. Actions aligned with your business goals are more likely to gain stakeholder buy-in and deliver measurable results. In my experience, when data initiatives tie into the bigger picture, they tend to receive the support they need.

Addressing Foundational Issues

Before diving into complex projects, you should address foundational issues like data quality, accessibility, and governance structures. These are the building blocks of advancing your data capabilities. With them, more advanced initiatives will likely gain traction. It's like trying to build a skyscraper on a shaky foundation - it won't stand the test of time.

Considering Employee Readiness and Engagement

Gauge your employees' readiness for change and focus on areas with the least resistance. Early wins in receptive departments can help build momentum, making rolling out data initiatives across the organisation easier. Remember, change is smoother when people are on board.

Leveraging Leadership Support

Leadership commitment is essential for success. Prioritise actions where leaders are most engaged. Strong leadership can help overcome resistance and provide the resources to push initiatives forward. I've seen projects run smoothly and succeed simply because leadership was fully behind them.

Evaluating Time Sensitivity

Lastly, consider any time-sensitive actions influenced by external factors like compliance requirements or market trends. Prioritise these to avoid unnecessary risks or missed opportunities. Sometimes, timing is everything.

Putting It All Together

When prioritising actionable steps to embed a data-driven mindset, begin by mapping each action based on its potential impact and effort. For quick wins, focus on high-impact, low-effort actions. For example, implementing user-friendly data visualisation tools can enhance data accessibility and empower employees to make data-driven decisions with minimal training.

At the same time, plan for high-impact, high-effort initiatives as part of your long-term strategy. These actions, such as developing data literacy programs, may require significant investment but will provide lasting value by elevating skills across your company. When you encounter low-impact, low-effort tasks, treat them as supplementary. They can be addressed if time and resources allow, but shouldn't divert attention from more critical actions.

Always consider organisational alignment and prioritise actions that support strategic goals. Address foundational issues first, such as improving data accessibility or establishing clear governance policies, as these provide the groundwork for other initiatives.

Assess employee readiness and identify teams most open to data-driven changes. Launching initiatives where resistance is low can cause early wins, generating momentum across the organisation. Finally, leverage leadership support by prioritising actions where leadership is most committed and evaluate time sensitivity to address compliance or market pressures.

Defining Milestones and Deliverables

Once you know which steps to take, it helps to set clear milestones and deliverables. Milestones mark important points in your plan where you can check how far you've come. Deliverables are the results you expect to produce at these points. By defining these in advance, you give everyone a clear idea of what to aim for and how to measure success.

Think about how you will know if you are reaching your goals. For example, you might decide that a certain part of your data should be accurate most of the time or that many employees should use a new data tool. Setting these kinds of goals helps everyone understand what they need to achieve. It also helps to plan regular times, such as monthly or quarterly reviews, to check if you are meeting these targets. During these check-ins, you can see what's working, what needs adjusting, and whether anything should change as the business grows and new information comes to light.

Staying flexible is important. As you learn more, you need to update your milestones or deliverables, so they better fit your changing needs. By being open to making changes along the way, you keep your data strategy strong, relevant, and ready to support the company's future.

This clear approach keeps everyone focused, moving forward, and working together toward shared results. By defining what success looks like, when it should happen, and how you will measure it, you create a path that guides your team through each stage of the data strategy journey. We'll look at these ideas more closely in the next chapter.

Structuring the Data Strategy Implementation Plan

Organising your data initiatives into a clear roadmap makes it easier for everyone to work together. By grouping related projects, understanding which ones depend on others, and connecting them with existing parts of the business, you create a path that saves time and helps the whole company move in the same direction. Instead of separate, scattered efforts, this approach ensures that every step supports your company's bigger goals.

Creating a Coherent Portfolio of Initiatives

When you group related data projects under common themes, it becomes easier to manage them and reach your goals. For example, you might have one set of projects focused on learning more about customers and another set aimed at making daily work smoother. By organising projects this way, you help teams with similar goals share knowledge, learn from each other, and move forward more quickly.

Once projects are grouped, it is important to understand how they depend on one another. Some tasks cannot begin until certain steps are finished. For instance, you may need to set up a data storage system before starting a new reporting process. By mapping these connections, you create a logical order of work. This clear sequence prevents delays and ensures everyone knows what to do next.

Each project should have a clearly named manager responsible for guiding the team, keeping track of progress, and solving problems. Knowing who is in charge helps everyone understand where to turn for answers. It also makes it easier to fix issues quickly, keep work on schedule, and ensure the entire set of data projects moves in the right direction.

Integrating with Corporate Functions

Your data projects should fit naturally with the work done by other parts of the company, such as IT and Finance. IT can provide the tools and technical support your data initiatives need. Finance can offer the funds and budgeting help required to keep projects running smoothly. By working closely with these departments, you make sure resources are ready when you need them, making your data work more efficiently and dependable.

Your data efforts depend on people, so you should also work closely with HR. If your projects require new skills, HR can help hire the right people or arrange training programs for current staff. By planning this early, you build a team that knows how to use data well and can handle new challenges as they come up. This way, your data projects remain strong and can grow along with the company.

Finally, make sure your data strategy does not stand apart from other important plans happening in the company. It should blend in smoothly, helping different teams share ideas and learn from each other. When data work supports and improves other efforts, the entire organisation benefits, making better decisions that lead to long-lasting success.

Engaging Stakeholders and Governance Bodies

Data strategies depend on people as much as they depend on tools and plans. By involving all levels of the organisation, such as those who lead teams, those who work on the front line, and those who guide overall direction, it helps data efforts run smoothly, bring real value, and keep improving over time.

Empowering Middle Management and Frontline Teams

Middle managers and frontline employees directly experience the changes that come with using data. By providing them with opportunities to share ideas and ask questions, you make it easier for everyone to speak up. You might hold regular meetings or set up simple online spaces for comments and suggestions. This approach keeps communication open and helps your team members feel involved.

It's beneficial to have data champions within each team and to have open communication. These trusted individuals understand the new tools and methods, allowing them to guide their coworkers, answer questions, and provide support. This support system makes it less confusing when new data practices are introduced.

Continuous learning is also essential. Offer training sessions, short lessons, or handy guides to build everyone's comfort with data. Over time, these efforts will raise the overall skill level of your teams. With proper guidance, supportive champions, and ongoing education, the people closest to the work can make the biggest difference in using data effectively.

Leveraging Data Governance Committees

Your data governance committees act as guardians of quality and fairness. They ensure that data is managed properly and that privacy rules are followed. By setting standards and monitoring compliance, these committees help prevent issues that could harm your company's reputation.

When disagreements or questions arise about roles and responsibilities, governance committees' step in to provide clarity. They resolve disputes, define roles, and ensure each data project stays on track. This fairness and oversight make it easier for everyone in your organisation to collaborate effectively.

As your company grows and regulations evolve, governance committees ensure that your data practices keep pace. They review and update guidelines, adapt to new laws, and suggest improvements when necessary. By doing so, they help your organisation stay prepared for future challenges and maintain robust data management practices.

Summary

In this chapter, we turned our focus from planning to doing. We explored how to take the ideas and goals from earlier steps and put them into action, making sure our data strategy becomes a strong part of everyday work. We learned how to pick the right projects by considering the impact, effort, and how well each idea fits the company's goals. We also looked at the importance of setting clear targets and timelines, so everyone knows what success looks like and how to measure it.

Beyond choosing what to do first, we discussed ways to organise data projects so they fit together smoothly and don't work against each other. We showed how to bring different parts of the company into the process, such as IT, Finance, and HR, so that data efforts have the right tools, funding, and people. We then explored how to involve everyone, from frontline teams to data committees, to make sure data insights are trusted, well-governed, and used to improve results.

By following these steps, you create a living, adaptable plan that keeps growing and changing as your company moves forward. With the right priorities, clear goals, strong teamwork, and proper oversight, your data strategy can flourish, helping the entire organisation make smarter decisions and reach its long-term objectives.

Chapter 9:
Measuring Success and Demonstrating ROI

Measuring the success of a data strategy helps everyone in your team understand if their efforts are working as planned. By relying on evidence, they can show that the strategy is worth the time and money spent. When a data strategy produces strong results, it gains trust, support, and the chance to continue growing. Without clear evidence, it is hard to prove its value, and people may lose interest or confidence in the work being done.

When looking at results, it is important to measure both clear, easy-to-count results and less obvious ones. Clear results might include higher revenue, lower costs, faster production, or better use of employees' time. Less obvious results might show up as stronger brand image, happier customers, more engaged staff, or a better environment for creating new products and services. By looking at both kinds of results, leaders can get a full idea of how the data strategy helps the business.

To show the return on investment, leaders should set goals and key performance indicators before they start. They should gather and study data often, share what they learn in simple ways, and listen to what employees, customers, and partners say about the changes they see. They can also compare their results to what other companies are doing, so everyone understands how well they are performing. This is not something done once and then forgotten. It is a regular process that helps guide improvements and keeps the data strategy on track as the business changes over time. By showing how well the data strategy works, leaders can keep support strong, protect past investments, and make it easier to try new data ideas later.

Importance of Measuring Impact

Measuring impact helps people make better choices. When they have real facts and figures, they do not have to guess. They know which projects to continue, which ones to change, and which ones to stop. This careful look at results gives everyone a clear picture of what is happening. It also helps groups stay honest about their work, because anyone can look at the numbers and see what has improved or where more work is needed.

When progress is easy to understand, people inside and outside the company feel more confident. If everyone can see that the data strategy is moving the business forward, it builds trust and encourages more people to join in. Keeping track of what works well and what does not makes it possible to correct problems quickly. Over time, this habit of learning from the results leads to better decisions, smarter plans, and stronger business growth.

Linking Data Initiatives to Business Goals

Data initiatives should fit closely with what the business wants to achieve. Each measurement should connect directly to a main company goal, so leaders can see how using data changes real business results. For example, if the company wants to reach new customers, then measurements should focus on how well it is doing at understanding those customers and selling to them. If the company wants to improve products, then the numbers should show how data is helping make those products more appealing or cost-effective.

It is also important to know the difference between everyday measurements and those that show big, long-term changes. Everyday measures might track if systems are working smoothly and if data is correct, while bigger measures might show how much more money the company earns because of a data-inspired idea. These measurements should not stay the same forever. As the business changes, the measurements should change too, making sure the company always keeps track of what matters most.

Establishing Meaningful KPIs and Metrics

Before measuring success, it is important to choose KPIs and metrics that clearly reflect what the business wants to achieve. When each KPI is easy to understand and closely tied to real goals, the business can turn data into helpful insights. By avoiding KPIs that do not matter and focusing on ones that give leaders what they need, the company sets itself up for better decisions at all levels.

Selecting Relevant Indicators

When picking which metric to track, focus on those that connect directly to the company's most important aims. These metrics should show clear progress toward goals like higher revenue, better customer satisfaction, or stronger market presence. If the data behind them is easy to get and regularly updated, everyone will trust the results.

Good KPIs also point to how the organisation can improve. For example, if the number of customers leaving rises, the team knows it must work on keeping them happier. If a certain group of sales leads never turns into paying customers, the team can refine its sales approach. It is wise to limit the number of measures used, focusing only on the few that truly matter and support the company's biggest goals.

When goals are specific, measurable, realistic, and time-bound, it is simpler to judge progress. As the company grows and changes, you should revisit the metrics you're focusing on to make sure they still help guide decisions. By choosing clear, useful, and easy-to-obtain indicators, leaders give their teams a strong path to follow and ensure everyone moves together toward long-term success.

Characteristics of Bad Metrics

Not all metrics are helpful. Some can cause confusion, waste time, or lead people away from the company's real goals. By knowing what makes a metric weak, leaders can avoid using numbers that do not help their teams make better decisions.

- **Subjective:** If a metric relies on personal opinions or lacks a clear, shared meaning, it becomes hard to understand and compare. For example, saying 'improve customer engagement' without defining what that means can lead to mixed ideas about success.

- **Irrelevant:** A metric that does not connect to the company's main goals creates unnecessary work and noise. If the company is focused on cutting costs, then measuring social media likes does not help, since it does not show if spending is going down or if money is being used more wisely.
- **Unactionable:** Some metrics show what has happened but do not suggest what to do next. If the numbers do not guide the team toward a solution or a better approach, they offer little value. Good metrics should help people know how to improve.
- **Complex:** When a metric is too hard to understand, filled with special terms or tricky math, it discourages people from using it. If the measure is not simple and clear, teams might ignore it or misunderstand what it means, which makes it useless.
- **Lagging:** Metrics that appear too late to influence current decisions can leave teams behind the curve. If market changes happen quickly, waiting months to see results does not help. Timely measures let leaders adjust their plans before it is too late.
- **Vanity:** Some numbers look impressive but do not reflect real business growth. Large website traffic or many followers can seem good, but they do not matter if they do not increase revenue, improve quality, or help the company reach important goals.
- **Misused:** Even a well-meant metric can be harmful if used for the wrong purpose. For example, using a measure of speed in one team to judge everyone's performance can push people to cut corners. Leaders must consider how a metric might lead to unwanted behaviour.

By avoiding these weak metrics, companies can focus on measures that truly support their strategy. Every chosen metric should be clear, tied to important goals, lead to action, and arrive at the right time. When metrics meet these standards, they provide real guidance for improvement and growth.

Characteristics of Good Metrics

Good metrics make it easier to see how well the company is doing, where it is heading, and what to do next. They help everyone understand the current situation, measure progress toward important goals, and act quickly when changes are needed.

- **Understandable:** They use clear language and simple terms that everyone can understand, even without a technical background. For example, 'Average Customer Response Time' is easy for any team member to follow.
- **Meaningful:** They connect directly to important goals, showing how progress in one area supports the company's larger aims. For example, tracking 'Net New Revenue from Data-Driven Offerings' clearly relates to growing the business.
- **Measurable:** They rely on reliable numbers that come from trustworthy sources, making it possible to measure changes over time. For example, using logs to track error rates in a data process gives clear, accurate data.
- **Responsive:** They are updated often enough that teams can make quick, informed decisions. This means checking key metrics at the right time, daily, weekly, or monthly, so adjustments can be made when it matters most.

Case Study: Choosing the Right KPIs at ASOS

ASOS, a UK-based online retailer, shows how selecting the right KPIs leads to real progress. By tracking customer engagement and sales trends in real time, ASOS saw a 20% boost in conversion rates within just six months. They focused on clear measures like cart abandonment rates, customer satisfaction scores, and daily sales figures. These numbers gave leaders an accurate view of what's working, making it easier to adjust inventory levels, respond quickly to market changes, and keep customers happy. As a result, ASOS improved not only their sales figures but also created a better shopping experience. This example shows that focusing on well-chosen metrics helps a company move in the right direction, remain flexible, and stay ahead of changing customer needs.

Summary

In this chapter, we learned why measuring the success of a data strategy is so important. By gathering real evidence about what works and what does not, leaders can show that their data efforts are truly helping the business. Measuring both clear, easy-to-track results, such as revenue growth or cost savings, and less obvious improvements, such as better teamwork or a stronger brand image, gives a complete view of how data drives progress. This approach helps build trust, earn ongoing support, and guide future plans as the business changes over time.

We also explored how to choose the right key performance indicators and metrics. Good metrics are simple, meaningful, and based on reliable information, making it easier for everyone to understand their purpose and take action. Bad metrics, on the other hand, can confuse teams, waste time, or push people away from real goals. By focusing on high-quality measures that connect directly to what the company wants to achieve, leaders can keep everyone moving in the right direction.

Overall, a strong measurement approach ensures that data investments pay off, keeps improvements steady, and supports smarter, faster decision-making. By regularly checking results, acting on what we learn, and making sure our measurements stay up-to-date, we can turn data into a powerful tool for lasting business success.

Chapter 10:
Future-Proofing Your Data Strategy

Building a data strategy is about more than just what you have done so far. It also means thinking ahead and preparing for changes that have yet to happen. Technology, rules, and business needs will keep shifting, so you must always be ready to update your approach.

If you wait until problems appear, you will waste time on re-work and fall behind. Stay out of trouble by assessing various potential scenarios and how to respond to each one. Keep track of new ideas, tools and rules, too. This way, you stay in control and can guide your company smoothly through big changes.

Treat your data strategy like something that can grow and evolve. Check it often, ask if it still fits your needs, and make changes when things no longer work. It should never feel old or stuck in the past.

If you do this, your company will stand strong today and tomorrow. By looking ahead and making careful changes, you can use data to make good decisions, reach your goals, and outpace others. Future-proofing means staying flexible, not guessing the future exactly. You prepare so that no matter what comes, you can handle it. By doing this, your data strategy will last a long time and continue to help your company succeed.

Maintaining a Forward-Looking Perspective

Looking ahead means planning not just for today's needs but also for what might come next. Start by setting clear goals for the future so your work will help you move towards them. Pick tools and platforms that can grow and change together with your business so you don't have to start from scratch each time something new appears.

Stay open to fresh ideas and encourage your team to experiment with new methods. Even if some attempts fail, they'll provide valuable lessons. Each experiment, successful or not, offers insights that help shape a stronger data strategy. Of course, it's important to balance resources, risk and reward. Create safe testing environments where your team can try new tools without jeopardizing critical systems. These low-risk experiments often lead to surprising improvements.

Keep an eye on new trends and technologies that might benefit you. Understanding where the world is headed helps you choose tools and approaches that won't become outdated. By keeping a forward-looking perspective, you ensure that your data strategy stays useful, up-to-date, and ready for anything the future might bring.

Staying Ahead with Emerging Technologies

Staying ahead means finding the right tools before your competitors do. As data grows and changes, new technologies will help you understand it faster and make smarter decisions. By watching your industry and the broader tech world, you can spot tools that improve how you collect, store, and use information. Choosing these technologies early on can keep your company agile and ready for whatever comes next.

The following sections highlight three emerging technologies you can consider and potentially include in your data strategy.

Artificial Intelligence and Machine Learning

Artificial intelligence (AI) and machine learning (ML) enable computers to learn from data and improve decisions over time. Popular large language models (LLMs), such as ChatGPT, can understand and generate human-like text after extensive training, making them versatile tools for answering questions, summarizing reports, drafting documents, and more. These capabilities help companies respond to customer inquiries, spot trends hidden in written feedback, and work more efficiently.

The potential gains stretch far beyond the conversation. AI and ML can forecast product demand, helping supply chain managers anticipate customer needs and stock the right items before their competitors do. In manufacturing, predictive maintenance models can detect when machinery is likely to fail, reducing downtime and saving money. This forward-looking approach strengthens an organization's position and builds long-term resilience. Over time, as these tools evolve and improve, savvy leaders who stay informed, refine their models, and adopt emerging best practices can maintain a competitive edge in a constantly changing marketplace.

Of course, AI and ML are not foolproof. They rely on good data. If the underlying information is outdated or biased, decisions will suffer. Even advanced models like LLMs may produce incorrect or misleading answers if not trained and monitored carefully. At the time of writing, many can still 'hallucinate' unreliable content. Without proper oversight, an initially helpful tool can start to 'drift', which means a drop in performance, becoming a source of costly errors, damaging trust and undermining performance.

The key is continuous improvement. Remain vigilant about data quality, regularly update and retrain models, and learn from others' successes and missteps. As regulations shift, data volumes grow, and customer expectations evolve, adaptability is essential. By refining AI and ML tools to stay accurate, fair, and relevant, companies can steadily transform technology-driven insights into long-term advantages.

Blockchain and Distributed Ledgers

Blockchain, the technology behind popular cryptocurrencies like Bitcoin and Ethereum, has been gaining significant momentum. At the time of writing, Bitcoin has just hit USD $100k. Instead of storing information in a single database, blockchain spreads data across many computers. This makes it extremely difficult to alter undetected records, which helps foster a trustworthy environment. Such integrity is especially beneficial in supply chains, where products pass through numerous hands and systems before reaching customers. With blockchain, each step, from raw material sourcing to factory assembly, shipping, and retail delivery, is recorded so all participants can independently verify. No single party can quietly modify the data to hide mistakes, counterfeit goods, or unethical sourcing. This transparency reduces disputes, prevents fraud, and ensures that everyone sees the same, accurate information.

Smart contracts and automated rules embedded within the blockchain further streamline this process. For example, when a payment is received, a smart contract can automatically transfer the title of the goods to the buyer, eliminating middlemen and lowering the chance of errors or delays. Still, blockchain is evolving. Some platforms need help to handle large-scale data or consume significant energy, and regulatory environments vary by region. Before rolling it out widely, it's wise to test blockchain on a small portion of the business to confirm its value, identify potential issues, and fine-tune processes. As tools improve, regulations become clearer, and businesses learn from early pilots, blockchain stands in a prime position to bring lasting improvements in data reliability, operational efficiency, and trust throughout supply chains and beyond.

Internet of Things

The Internet of Things (IoT) extends connectivity to everyday objects, from factory equipment and delivery trucks to home appliances, allowing them to generate and share data in real-time. This constant stream of information can reshape entire operations. For example, sensors on industrial machines can alert you before a critical part fails, preventing costly downtime. Delivery vehicles can continuously transmit their locations, helping logistics teams optimize routes, improve on-time performance, and enhance the overall supply chain experience.

When implemented thoughtfully, IoT can drive smarter decisions and continuous improvement. By analysing data patterns, businesses might fine-tune store layouts to guide customers through a more satisfying shopping experience or adjust production schedules based on actual equipment usage. Over time, these insights help companies stay flexible, reduce waste, and move quickly to meet shifting market demands.

However, IoT brings unique challenges. As devices become more widely adopted, the volume of incoming data can overwhelm existing storage and analysis systems if not planned properly. Without solid infrastructure, data that could have provided valuable insights may become confusing. Security is another priority. More connected devices mean more potential entry points for cyberattacks. Strong safeguards and regular audits are essential to maintain trust and protect sensitive information.

It often pays to start small. Connect a limited set of devices, learn from the data, and refine your processes before scaling up. This phased approach builds confidence, reveals what works, and highlights what needs improvement. As IoT matures and businesses gain experience, they can manage growing data streams more effectively, strengthen security, and apply their lessons across broader operations.

Ultimately, as connectivity becomes the norm, IoT stands to transform how companies' sense and respond to their environments. By investing in careful planning, strong security, and capable data management, organizations can harness IoT to remain agile, informed, and ready for the future, turning steady data flows into lasting success.

Anticipating Regulatory and Market Changes

As technology grows, the rules and market conditions around it also change. Keeping an eye on new laws, ethical standards, and competitors' actions helps your data strategy stay up-to-date and effective. This proactive approach reduces risks and ensures that your strategy meets the needs of everyone involved in your business.

Proactive Compliance

Laws and regulations about data are always changing. By staying ahead of these changes, your company can avoid mistakes that might cost money and build trust with customers and partners.

Watching for new laws is very important. Just following the current rules isn't enough because new ones keep coming. For example, many new privacy laws started appearing worldwide after the GDPR law was introduced in 2018. In 2024, 20 US states will have their own data privacy laws, and more will be created. This shows that data privacy is becoming more important, and businesses must stay alert.

To keep up with these changes, you might set up a special team to watch for new regulations or use software that tracks legal updates. These tools can help you learn about important changes early to prepare for them. It's like having a system that alerts you when the weather is about to change, helping you stay ready.

Updating your policies regularly is also key. When new laws come out, your data rules must adapt and change. This isn't something you do once; it's a continuous process. For example, the European Data Protection Board often updates guidelines on how to follow GDPR. By keeping your policies current, you ensure that your company always meets the latest standards.

Having a clear process for managing regulatory changes is very helpful. This means having steps to track, evaluate, and respond to new laws. Assigning specific people to handle these changes ensures that nothing is missed and that your company can quickly adapt. It's like having a plan that helps you respond quickly when the weather suddenly changes.

Managing risks is another important part of proactive compliance. You should plan what to do if there is a data breach or you accidentally break a law. These plans should include steps to fix the problem, inform the right people, and work with authorities to resolve the issue.

Using technology can make managing these risks easier. Tools that constantly check your data activities can help you find and fix compliance problems before they become serious. This is like having a security system that alerts you to even small issues before they become big problems.

Proactive compliance is not just about avoiding fines; it's about earning trust. When customers and partners see that your company takes data protection seriously, they are more likely to trust you. In a world where data breaches are common, showing that you are committed to keeping data safe can give your business a big advantage.

As you build your proactive compliance strategy, here are some practical steps to consider:

1. Regularly check how your data practices might affect privacy and fix any risks you find.
2. Use systems that manage customer permissions to ensure you respect their choices and follow laws like the GDPR.
3. Stay informed about upcoming data privacy laws and prepare for them in advance.
4. Use data analysis to predict future regulatory changes based on past trends.

By being proactive with compliance, your company can turn it into a strength instead of a problem. This means being ready for any new laws or market changes and ensuring your data strategy stays strong and effective no matter what happens.

Adapting to Shifting Markets

Markets are always changing. New technologies come out, what customers like can shift, and the economy can go up or down. To stay successful, your business must be flexible and ready to adjust when these changes happen.

One important way to keep up with the market is through competitive benchmarking. This means regularly comparing how your company is doing against others in your industry. Doing this lets you see what your competitors are doing well and where you can improve. For example, if you notice a competitor using a new data tool that makes them work faster, you might also want to try that tool. This helps you stay on track and find ways to be better than others.

Benchmarking should be something you do all the time, not just once. Start by determining the key things that show how well your company performs. Then, collect information about these things from both your company and your competitors. Look at the data to find out where you are doing well and where you can do better. Based on what you find, set goals that are realistic and achievable. After making changes, keep an eye on how things are going to make sure your improvements are working.

Another way to stay ahead is by having flexible strategies. This means being ready to change your plans quickly if something unexpected happens. For example, when the COVID pandemic started, many businesses switched to online operations to keep running. If your company has flexible strategies, you can make these changes smoothly without too much trouble.

Regularly review and update your data plans to build flexibility in your strategies. Create backup plans for different situations, like economic downturns or sudden changes in customer preferences. Encourage your team to think creatively and be open to trying new ideas. Invest in technologies that can grow and change with your business needs so you don't have to start from scratch every time something new comes up.

Strategic partnerships are also very helpful. You can share knowledge and resources by working with other companies, research institutions, or industry groups. These partnerships can give you new ideas and help you stay informed about the latest trends and changes in the market. For instance, partnering with a tech company might provide you early access to new data tools to improve your operations. Similarly, joining a data privacy group can help you understand and prepare for new regulations.

Find partners that share your goals and values to make the most of strategic partnerships. Set clear objectives for what you want to achieve together and keep open lines of communication. Regularly check how each partnership is helping your business and adjust as needed to ensure they continue to provide value.

By combining competitive benchmarking, flexible strategies, and strategic partnerships, your business can navigate market changes more effectively. This approach helps you stay relevant and take advantage of new opportunities before your competitors do. In the world of data strategy, being able to adapt quickly and smartly is what will keep your company ahead and thriving.

Creating Enduring Value

Making sure your data strategy stays useful over time is not something you do just once. It requires checking your plans now and then, making changes based on new lessons, and encouraging everyone to stay open-minded and ready to adjust. By doing this, your company keeps using data in a way that stays helpful and valuable even as the world changes.

Periodic Strategic Refreshes

Looking at your data strategy regularly helps it stay in line with what your business needs and what is happening in the market. By doing this, you catch problems early and keep improving. For example, you might review your plan every six months or once a year. During these reviews, ask if your main goals and numbers still make sense. If they do not, decide what to change, so your strategy keeps moving you toward success.

When you do these reviews, include different people. Leaders, employees, customers, and partners can all share ideas you might have missed. For example, a store manager might have noticed that customers care more and more about carbon emissions. This new idea might lead you to collect and analyse carbon data to adjust your plans and stay ahead of customers' expectations.

Always learn from what happens, whether it is good or bad. If a data project does not work well, try to understand why. Maybe the numbers were incorrect, or your team used them incorrectly. By looking closely, you learn what to fix. Each time you find and solve a problem, your strategy becomes stronger and more useful.

As you review and refresh your strategy, remember to use your data wisely and pay attention to changes in your industry. Stay open to using new tools, like improved AI programs or better data management methods. Check that the quality of your data is still good and that your rules for handling it still make sense. By working this way, you keep your strategy active, helpful, and always ready for what comes next.

Sustaining a Future-Ready Culture

To keep your data strategy strong over time, creating a culture that looks ahead and welcomes change is important. One way to do this is by building skills at all levels. This does not mean just teaching people how to read charts but helping them understand how data can guide better decisions and lead to new ideas. Training should not be a one-time event because technology and best practices change quickly. By offering ongoing lessons and workshops, everyone can stay current and confident in handling data.

Encouraging people to try new things is another way to prepare your culture for the future. Set up safe and supportive places where teams can test ideas without fear of failing. Companies like Google have let employees spend part of their work time exploring new projects that might one day become great products. Allowing this kind of experimentation shows that you value fresh thinking, even if only some ideas succeed immediately. Over time, this leads to a more creative and energetic workforce.

Having leaders who support data-driven thinking is also key. Leaders should show that they rely on data when making decisions and explain why this matters for the company. They should give teams the resources they need, even when times are tough, and ensure that data remains part of the company's long-term goals. When people see their leaders treating data as important, they will do the same.

It can help to name certain employees as 'data champions.' These champions come from different parts of the company and work together to spread data skills and encourage the careful use of data tools. They can act as a bridge between technical experts and other teams, ensuring everyone feels included and can benefit from data.

Building a future-ready culture never really ends. Check-in from time to time by asking employees how they feel about the changes, looking at whether people are using data in their daily tasks, and noticing if your data projects bring good results. Use what you learn to improve your approach. As long as you stay focused on skill growth, trying new methods, and keeping leaders involved, your company will be ready to adapt to whatever comes next and keep getting value from your data strategy.

Summary

This chapter explored how to prepare your data strategy to handle whatever the future brings. Instead of treating it like a one-time plan, we looked at ways to keep it flexible, fresh, and ready for new changes in technology, rules, and the market.

We saw that staying ahead means more than just watching trends. It involves actively choosing the right tools, such as AI and IoT, to gain an edge. It also means carefully handling new methods like blockchain to improve trust and reduce errors. We discussed the importance of following new laws and adjusting quickly when the market shifts. Most importantly, we learned that your organization's culture should always encourage learning, testing new ideas, and strong support from leaders. By regularly checking your strategy, improving your skills, and listening to different voices within your company, you keep your data approach powerful and long-lasting.

All these steps ensure that you do not simply react to change; you shape it. By future-proofing your data strategy, you set a path to help your company stay strong, confident, and ready to grow, no matter what tomorrow brings.

Conclusion

As we reach the end of this journey through *The Strategic Data Playbook*, it's clear that the true power of data lies in its strategic application. Throughout the chapters, we've examined how data can shift from a passive, often underutilised resource into a central driver of growth, innovation, and competitive advantage. The lessons learned include:

1. Understanding what data strategy is
2. Aligning it with business objectives
3. Assessing data maturity
4. Cultivating a data-driven culture
5. Establishing effective processes
6. Empowering people
7. Leveraging the right technologies
8. Executing plans
9. Measuring success
10. Preparing for the future

All these concepts build toward a more impactful way of working with data.

More importantly, we've explored a comprehensive six-step data strategy framework designed to guide you through this transformation:

Step 1: Define Business Objectives and Align Data Initiatives: In Chapters 1 and 2, we saw how understanding and aligning your data goals with broader business objectives ensures that data efforts deliver meaningful value rather than becoming isolated data projects.

Step 2: Assess Your Organisation's Data Landscape: Chapter 3 provided insights into evaluating your current data maturity. By honestly assessing where you stand, you set a clear baseline for growth, helping you chart a path toward more advanced capabilities and strategic decision-making.

Step 3: Grow a Data-Driven Culture: Chapters 4 and 5 highlighted the importance of mindset and people. By cultivating a culture that respects data-driven thinking and empowering teams to develop new skills, share knowledge, and embrace change, you enable everyone in the organisation to contribute to data initiatives.

Step 4: Develop Effective Processes: In Chapter 6, we focused on building robust processes, governance structures, and accountability measures. With reliable processes, data can flow more smoothly through your organisation, making it easier to trust and leverage information for strategic decisions.

Step 5: Empower Your People with the Right Tools and Technology: Chapter 7 emphasised selecting flexible, scalable technologies that support data accessibility, performance, and innovation. Choosing the right tools and approaches enables self-service analytics and ensures teams can find, analyse, and act on data quickly and efficiently.

Step 6: Execute and Sustain: Finally, Chapters 8 through 10 taught us how to translate plans into action, measure results, and future-proof your strategy. By starting with the highest-impact projects, collaborating across departments, and establishing clear metrics and KPIs, you create a feedback loop that constantly refines and strengthens your data strategy. By remaining adaptable and embracing new technologies, regulations, and market shifts, you ensure your data strategy remains a lasting source of competitive advantage.

As you implement these steps into practice, remember that building a truly data-driven organisation is not a one-time project but an ongoing journey. Your data strategy should evolve as your business grows, new technologies emerge, and market dynamics shift. Continuously learning from your data initiatives, celebrating successes, analysing setbacks, and refining your approach will keep your data strategy fresh and forward-looking.

You now have a structured blueprint to guide your efforts. You can harness data's full potential by aligning with objectives, assessing where you stand, nurturing a supportive culture, setting up strong processes, deploying the right tools, and executing effectively. Your organisation can become more agile, innovative, and resilient in the face of change. Take the insights you've gained here and lead your company toward a future where data shapes every decision, supports every strategy, and unlocks possibilities limited only by your own vision and ambition.

References

"Developing data strategy: a framework for success | Grant Thornton." Grant Thornton UK LLP, Nikhil Asthana, 4 Mar. 2021, https://www.grantthornton.co.uk/insights/developing-data-strategy-a-framework-for-success/

"A data strategy framework | Tableau." Tableau, https://www.tableau.com/en-gb/learn/articles/data-strategy-framework

"Design your data strategy in six steps | IBM." IBM, https://www.ibm.com/think/insights/data-differentiator/data-driven-organisation

"Defining a data strategy: An essential component of your transformation journey." DXC Technology, Srijani Dey, https://dxc.com/us/en/insights/perspectives/paper/defining-a-data-strategy

"What is Data Strategy? - Data Strategy Explained - AWS." Amazon Web Services, Inc., https://aws.amazon.com/what-is/data-strategy/

"Sunday Brunch: the Post Office scandal - a failure of operational governance." The Sustainable Investor, Dr Mimi Ajibade, 01 Jul. 2024, https://www.thesustainableinvestor.org.uk/the-post-office-scandal-a-failure-of-operational-governance/

"Post Office Horizon scandal: Why hundreds were wrongly prosecuted." BBC News, 30 Jul. 2024, https://www.bbc.co.uk/news/business-56718036

"What the Post Office Scandal teaches us about data and technology. " PLMR, Alex Hackett, 10 Jan. 2024, https://plmr.co.uk/2024/01/what-the-post-office-scandal-teaches-us-about-digital-and-data/

"Post Office Horizon scandal explained: Everything you need to know." ComputerWeekly.com, Karl Flinders, 08 Dec. 2024, https://www.computerweekly.com/feature/Post-Office-Horizon-scandal-explained-everything-you-need-to-know

"Fujitsu loses £50m in sales after Post Office scandal furore ." ComputerWeekly.com, Karl Flinders, 17 Sep. 2024, https://www.computerweekly.com/news/366610815/Fujitsu-loses-50m-in-sales-after-Post-Office-scandal-furore

"From iconic punchline: Blockbuster's CMO reflects on how things imploded. " Marketing Week, Thomas Hobbs, 3 Jul. 2017, https://www.marketingweek.com/blockbusters-cmo-failure/

"Unraveling Blockbuster's Digital Downfall and Lessons for Businesses in the Streaming Era." Factr | DataPeak, Smarter Data Management, Insights & No-Code Automation, https://www.factr.me/blog/blockbuster-bankruptcy

"Blockbuster's Business Model Bust." Thinkers360, Andrew Constable, Mar. 2021, https://www.thinkers360.com/tl/blog/members/blockbusters-business-model-bust

"A Look Back At Why Blockbuster Really Failed And Why It Didn't Have To." Forbes, Greg Satell, 10 Dec. 2021, https://www.forbes.com/sites/gregsatell/2014/09/05/a-look-back-at-why-blockbuster-really-failed-and-why-it-didnt-have-to/

"Artificial Intelligence in Business - 10 Key Questions for your company." Nexus Integra, https://nexusintegra.io/artificial-intelligence-in-business/

"Guide: How to align an organisation to define a data strategy - data.org." data.org, 05 Apr. 2024, https://data.org/guides/how-to-align-an-organisation-to-define-a-data-strategy/

"4 Ways Change Management Is Key to Effective Data Governance Adoption | Informatica." Informatica, Melanie Parker-Barnes, 5 Oct. 2023, https://www.informatica.com/blogs/4-ways-change-management-is-key-to-effective-data-governance-adoption.html

"4 Ways to Align Your Data Strategy with the Business." Modal Learning, Jennifer Juo, 29 Aug. 2024, https://www.modallearning.com/blog-posts/4-ways-to-align-your-data-strategy-with-the-business

"The Three Levels of Strategy: Corporate, Business and Functional Strategy." Digital Leadership, Stefan F.Dieffenbacher, 23 Apr. 2024, https://digitalleadership.com/blog/levels-of-strategy/

"Overcoming Common Challenges in Data Strategy Implementation" Gary Allemann, https://www.masterdata.co.za/index.php/implementing-a-data-strategy-best-practices/data-strategy-challenges

"How To Overcome Common Data Integration Challenges." DotActiv, 8 May. 2024, https://www.dotactiv.com/blog/data-integration-challenges

"11+ Most Common Data Integration Challenges & Solutions." Estuary, 31 Jul. 2023, https://estuary.dev/data-integration-challenges/

"Enterprises are collecting more data, but do they know what to do with it?" ZDNET, Stephanie Condon, 15 Jul. 2024, https://www.zdnet.com/home-and-office/sustainability/4-ways-the-tech-we-buy-is-designed-to-fail-and-why-you-should-be-furious/

"BBC iPlayer is "Fastest Growing VOD Platform in the UK"." IBC, 18 Sept. 2024, https://www.ibc.org/news/bbc-iplayer-is-fastest-growing-vod-platform-in-the-uk/12126.article

"Key data on I love my Tesco Clubcard loyalty program in Central Europe, the Republic of Ireland, and in the United Kingdom (UK) as of February 2024." Statista, https://www.statista.com/statistics/1400244/tesco-clubcard-data/

"ROLLS-ROYCE: A Circular Economy Business Model Case." Core, Aleyn Smith-Gillespie, Ana Muñoz, Doug Morwood, Tiphaine Aries, 1 Jan. 2018, https://core.ac.uk/outputs/322910261/

"Rolls-Royce's Customer Service and Aftermarket Services - The Case Centre." The Case Centre, The Case Centre, 2020, https://www.thecasecentre.org/products/view?id=168501

"Annual Report 2023 – Rolls-Royce Holdings plc." Rolls-Royce Holdings plc, 2023, https://www.rolls-royce.com/~/media/Files/R/Rolls-Royce/documents/annual-report/2024/2023-annual-report.pdf

"Creating a Data Maturity Model: What, Why, How - DATAVERSITY." DATAVERSITY, Keith D. Foote, 29 Oct. 2024, https://www.dataversity.net/creating-a-data-maturity-model-what-why-how/

"What is data maturity? — Data Orchard." Data Orchard, https://www.dataorchard.org.uk/what-is-data-maturity

"What is Data Maturity & How to Climb the Data Maturity Scale?." SoftKraft, Henryk Konsek, https://www.softkraft.co/what-is-data-maturity-and-how-to-climb-the-data-maturity-scale/

"The four stages of data maturity–and how to ace them | Heap." Heap, Rachel Obstler, 3 Apr. 2023, https://www.heap.io/blog/the-four-stages-of-data-maturity

"The Human Impact of Data Literacy." Accenture, 2020, https://www.accenture.com/content/dam/accenture/final/a-com-migration/r3-3/pdf/pdf-118/accenture-the-human-impact-data-literacy.pdf

"Coca-Cola Andina Boosts Efficiency and Customer Satisfaction with Analytics on AWS | Case Study | AWS." Amazon Web Services, Inc., 2024, https://aws.amazon.com/solutions/case-studies/coca-cola-andina-analytics-case-study/

"Palantir Technologies + Scuderia Ferrari Partnership Overview." Palantir, 2020, https://www.palantir.com/build/files/scuderia-ferrari-whitepaper.pdf

"The Data-Driven Mindset." L.E.K. Consulting LLC, Tom Diplock, Philip Roux, Philip Meier, https://www.lek.com/sites/default/files/insights/pdf-attachments/L.E.K._EI_Data-Driven%20Mindset_Final-2.pdf

"Does Your Data & Analytics Strategy Have These 10 Crucial Elements?." Forbes, Ganes Kesari, 03 Jun. 2024, https://www.forbes.com/sites/ganeskesari/2022/05/31/does-your-data--analytics-strategy-have-these-10-crucial-elements/

"Why Change Management Skills Are Essential To Data-Driven Success." Forbes, Brent Dykes, 01 Dec. 2022, https://www.forbes.com/sites/brentdykes/2022/11/29/why-change-management-skills-are-essential-to-data-driven-success/

"Data literacy for leaders | MIT Sloan." MIT Sloan, Sara Brown, 23 Jan. 2023, https://mitsloan.mit.edu/ideas-made-to-matter/data-literacy-leaders

"Developing a Data Literacy Program for Your Organization." DATAVERSITY, Paramita (Guha) Ghosh, 31 Jan. 2024, https://www.dataversity.net/developing-a-data-literacy-program-for-your-organisation/

"Data Quality Policy." NHS Yorkshire Ambulance Service, Head of Business Intelligence, Mar. 2021, https://www.yas.nhs.uk/media/3651/po-data-quality-policy-v61.pdf

"Crafting Effective Communication Strategies for Data Transformation Success." Cambridge Spark, Cambridge Spark, 25 Oct. 2024, https://www.cambridgespark.com/info/data-transformation-communication-strategy

"How to empower teams with analytics: data-driven culture." The Statsig Team, 23 Jul. 2024, https://www.statsig.com/perspectives/how-to-empower-teams-with-analytics-data-driven-culture

"The Importance of Data Driven Decision Making in Business." RIB Software, 6 Jun. 2024, https://www.rib-software.com/en/blogs/data-driven-decision-making-in-businesses

"Building trust in analytics." KPMG, Global Data & Analytics, https://assets.kpmg.com/content/dam/kpmg/ie/pdf/2019/03/ie-building-trust-in-analytics-data.pdf

"Best practices for establishing trust in data in a digital age: The critical role of verified trustworthy information." Moody's, 11 Sep. 2024, https://www.moodys.com/web/en/us/kyc/resources/insights/best-practices-establishing-trust-data-digital-age-critical-role-verified-trustworthy-information.html

"How to Cultivate a Data-Driven Culture in Your Organization." 180 Ops, AI Team, 20 May. 2024, https://www.180ops.com/180-perspective-change/how-to-cultivate-data-driven-culture-in-organisation

"Overcome Your Company's Resistance to Data." Harvard Business Review, Thomas C. Redman, 17 Apr. 2024, https://hbr.org/2015/03/overcome-your-companys-resistance-to-data

"DBS equips employees with skills to become everyday 'Data Heroes'." DBS https://www.dbs.com/newsroom/DBS_equips_employees_with_skills_to_become_everyday_Data_Heroes

"Chronic Data Skills Shortage costing UK £57.2 billion each year - Silicon Scotland." Silicon Scotland, 23 Aug. 2024, https://siliconscotland.com/chronic-data-skills-shortage-costing-uk-57-2-billion-each-year-2/

"Quantifying the UK Data Skills Gap - Full report - GOV.UK." GOV.UK, Department for Science, Innovation and Technology, 18 May. 2021, https://www.gov.uk/government/publications/quantifying-the-uk-data-skills-gap/quantifying-the-uk-data-skills-gap-full-report

"How to carry out an employee skills assessment | Brightmine." Brightmine UK, Natasha K. A. Wiebusch, 29 May. 2024, https://www.brightmine.com/uk/resources/guides-how-to/how-to-carry-out-an-employee-skills-assessment/

"How to Launch a Successful Data Literacy Program." Alteryx, https://www.alteryx.com/resources/e-book/how-to-launch-a-successful-data-literacy-program

"Data Literacy Program: Training, Consulting & Resources | Qlik." Qlik, https://www.qlik.com/us/services/data-literacy-program

"Using Mentoring As A Critical Employee Retention Tool." Mentorloop, Grace Winstanely, 8 Feb. 2023, https://mentorloop.com/blog/mentoring-employee-lifecycle-retention/

"Enhancing Employee Engagement With Data-Driven Insights." HireRoad, https://hireroad.com/resources/enhancing-employee-engagement-with-data-driven-insights

"What's it like to work at Amazon?." US About Amazon, Amazon Staff, 09 Feb. 2021, https://www.aboutamazon.com/news/workplace/an-insider-look-at-amazons-culture-and-processes

"How Clear Career Paths Strengthen Retention—and Diversity | Bain & Company." Bain, Julie Coffman, Elyse Rosenblum, Andrea D'Arcy, Laura Thompson Love, 23 Nov. 2021, https://www.bain.com/insights/how-clear-career-paths-strengthen-retention-and-diversity/

" Mentoring program case studies – results of mentoring in companies." Mentiway, Jacek Tkaczuk, https://mentiway.com/en/mentoring-program-case-studies-results-of-mentoring-in-companies/

"Building a Data Governance Strategy in 7 Steps." Aaron Bradshaw, 16 Dec. 2021, https://www.alation.com/blog/steps-for-building-data-governance-strategy/

"The Core Principles of Data Governance | Data Meaning." Data Meaning, 7 May. 2024, https://datameaning.com/2024/05/07/data-governance-principles/

"Data Sharing Governance Framework - GOV.UK." GOV.UK, Central Digital and Data Office, 23 May. 2022, https://www.gov.uk/government/publications/data-sharing-governance-framework/data-sharing-governance-framework

"Data Governance and Data Policies at the European Commission." European Commission, Secreteriat-General, Jul. 2020, https://commission.europa.eu/system/files/2020-07/summary-data-governance-data-policies_en.pdf

"Data Integrity vs. Data Quality: All the Differences." Astera, Zoha Shakoor, 30 Apr. 2024, https://www.astera.com/type/blog/data-integrity-vs-data-quality/

"How Uber Achieves Operational Excellence in the Data Quality Experience." Uber Blog, 5 Aug. 2021, https://www.uber.com/en-GB/blog/operational-excellence-data-quality/

"Case studies | ICO." ICO, https://ico.org.uk/for-organisations/advice-and-services/audits/data-protection-audit-framework/case-studies/

"Data Strategy: Why it Matters and How to Build One | Databricks Blog." Databricks, Josh Howard, Amit Kara, 09 Oct. 2024, https://www.databricks.com/blog/data-strategy-why-it-matters-and-how-build-one

"Data Strategy - Implement quick wins and create a scalable strategy that aligns to strategic business goals." Data Technology, https://datatechnology.co.uk/data-strategy

"Building Scalable Data Architectures: Principles and Best Practices." TimeXtender, Aaron Powers, 29 Aug. 2023, https://www.timextender.com/blog/product-technology/building-scalable-data-architectures-principles-and-best-practices

"The Need for Flexible Data Management: Why Is Data Flexibility So Important? - DATAVERSITY." DATAVERSITY, David Leivesley, 16 Dec. 2020, https://www.dataversity.net/the-need-for-flexible-data-management-why-is-data-flexibility-so-important/

"On-Premises vs Cloud: Key Differences & Which is Best for Your Business?." Cloud Panel, Nikita S., 19 Sep. 2023, https://www.cloudpanel.io/blog/on-premises-vs-cloud-computing/

"How to Create a Successful Data Integration Strategy? - Rivery." Rivery, Chen Cuello, 13 Sept. 2023, https://rivery.io/data-learning-center/data-integration-strategy/

"What is Self-Service Analytics?." IBM, Ivan Belcic, Cole Stryker, 4 Sep. 2024, https://www.ibm.com/think/topics/self-service-analytics

"Self-Service Analytics: Pros and Cons - DATAVERSITY." DATAVERSITY, Paramita (Guha) Ghosh, 08 Oct. 2024, https://www.dataversity.net/self-service-analytics-pros-and-cons/

"8 case studies and real world examples of how Big Data has helped keep on top of competition - Systems plus." Systems Plus, 09 Jun. 2023, https://systems-plus.com/8-case-studies-and-real-world-examples-of-how-big-data-has-helped-keep-on-top-of-competition/

"DataOps Engineering Explained — Real-World Cases from Airbnb, Netflix, Capital One, HomeGoods Plus." CDO Magazine, Ekambar Kumar Singirikonda, https://www.cdomagazine.tech/opinion-analysis/dataops-engineering-explained-real-world-cases-from-airbnb-netflix-capital-one-homegoods-plus

"Migrating from Data Centers to AWS | Capital One Case Study | AWS." Amazon Web Services, Inc., 2020, https://aws.amazon.com/solutions/case-studies/capital-one-all-in-on-aws/

"AT&T Provides Faster Insights at Lower Costs with Snowflake." Snowflake, https://www.snowflake.com/en/customers/all-customers/case-study/att/

"Data Strategy: A Complete Beginner's Guide for Everything You Need to Know About Building Your Data Strategy." Beyond: PDTW, Beyond Team, 01 Jul. 2024, https://www.puttingdatatowork.com/post/data-strategy-a-complete-beginner-s-guide-for-everything-you-need-to-know-about-building-your-data

"What is Data Strategy? Develop Yours in 10 Key Steps | Qlik ." Qlik, https://www.qlik.com/us/data-management/data-strategy

"The Dynamic Role of Middle Management in Modern Organizations." C-Suite Strategy, Rhys Fitzgerald, 10 Dec. 2024, https://www.c-suite-strategy.com/blog/the-dynamic-role-of-middle-management-in-modern-organizations

"Data Governance Committee 101: When Do You Need One?." Atlan, 28 Sep. 2024, https://atlan.com/data-governance-committee/

"What is a Key Performance Indicator (KPI)." SimpleKPI.com, Stuart Kinsey, 01 Mar. 2024, https://www.simplekpi.com/Resources/Key-Performance-Indicators

"HOW TO DEVELOP KPIS / PERFORMANCE MEASURES - KPI.org." KPI.org, Jason Harlow, 17 Apr. 2024, https://www.kpi.org/kpi-basics/kpi-development/

"How to build a data architecture to drive innovation—today and tomorrow | McKinsey." McKinsey & Company, Antonio Castro, 03 Jun. 2020, https://www.mckinsey.com/capabilities/mckinsey-digital/our-insights/how-to-build-a-data-architecture-to-drive-innovation-today-and-tomorrow

"Key Roles of Machine Learning in Data Analytics 2025 - Carmatec." Carmatec Inc - Mobile App Development Company, Nikhil, 20 Nov. 2024, https://www.carmatec.com/blog/key-roles-of-machine-learning-in-data-analytics/

"Mastering the 7 Principles of Privacy by Design for Compliance." Secure Privacy, https://secureprivacy.ai/blog/mastering-privacy-by-design-guide

"Guide to Competitive Benchmarking: Overview, Steps & FAQs." Dovetail, Dovetail Editorial Team, 03 Apr. 2024, https://dovetail.com/market-research/competitor-benchmarking/

"How to build a profitable data business | McKinsey." McKinsey & Company, Ari Libarikian, 18 Jul. 2024, https://www.mckinsey.com/capabilities/mckinsey-digital/our-insights/from-raw-data-to-real-profits-a-primer-for-building-a-thriving-data-business

"Creating Value from Data: Why you need to take a strategic approach to maximise the value of your data | Strategy&." PwC, PricewaterhouseCoopers, 2019, https://www.strategyand.pwc.com/gx/en/insights/2019/creating-value-from-data.html

"What is Data Literacy and Why is It Important: 8 Reasons." Atlan, 18 Oct. 2023, https://atlan.com/what-is-data-literacy-and-why-is-it-important/

"Data-driven companies: four compelling case studies - CodeStringers." CodeStringers, Michael Manzo, 05 Mar. 2024, https://www.codestringers.com/insights/data-driven-companies-four-compelling-case-studies/

"The Role of Feedback Loops in Shaping Organizational Culture ." vorecol.com, https://vorecol.com/blogs/blog-the-role-of-feedback-loops-in-shaping-organizational-culture-183609

About the Author

Wissen Lau is a distinguished data analytics expert and entrepreneur with a passion for leveraging technology to unlock productivity. A Warwick Business School graduate, Wissen has driven significant advancements in data analytics and AI automation, making substantial contributions to the industry.

At the largest rail company in the UK, Wissen developed an innovative algorithm and dashboard that saved £30 million in maintenance costs over the next 4 years. This achievement earned a prestigious Gold Award for the project, along with a Silver Award for his personal contributions. He also led the creation of the first-ever data quality dashboard. The data initiative reduced data quality issues by 10% in its first year, justified increased headcount, and became a strategic tool in regulatory compliance. In addition to his corporate achievements, Wissen ranked in the top 2% of a Kaggle competition, further demonstrating his advanced data science skills.

Wissen's entrepreneurial ventures include launching a successful web design business, generating £12,000 per month within its first year, as well as building and selling multiple profitable e-commerce stores.

Driven by a deep interest in AI automation and data-driven decision-making, Wissen continues to explore innovative ways to harness technology for greater productivity and industry impact.

For enquiries, consulting, or collaboration on data initiatives, please reach out via hello@wissenlau.com or by using the contact form in my website: wissenlau.com.

Thank you so much for making it to the end!

I really appreciate the time you took to read till the end of the book. As a small, individual publisher, it means a lot and I hope to make a positive impact for you and your company.

If you have 60 seconds, it'll mean the world to me if you share your honest feedback on Amazon. It does wonders for the book, and I love hearing your thoughts and experience with it!

To leave your feedback:

1) Open your camera app.
2) Point your mobile device at the QR code below.
3) This will open a review page in your browser app.

OR

Visit Link: wissenlau.com/sdp-feedback

THANK YOU!

www.ingramcontent.com/pod-product-compliance
Lightning Source LLC
Chambersburg PA
CBHW071051240526
45471CB00015B/1544